Supporting Trans People in Libraries

Supporting Trans People in Libraries

Stephen G. Krueger

LIBRARIES
UNLIMITED®

An Imprint of ABC-CLIO, LLC

Santa Barbara, California • Denver, Colorado

Library of Congress Cataloging-in-Publication Control Number: 2019022741

ISBN: 978-1-4408-6705-7 (paperback)
      978-1-4408-6706-4 (ebook)

23 22 21 20 19   1 2 3 4 5

This book is also available as an eBook.

Libraries Unlimited
An Imprint of ABC-CLIO, LLC

ABC-CLIO, LLC
147 Castilian Drive
Santa Barbara, California 93117
www.abc-clio.com

This book is printed on acid-free paper ∞

Manufactured in the United States of America

Community Voices icon is "customer reviews by Vectors Market from the Noun Project"; Personal Experiences icon is "Worker by James Fenton from the Noun Project"; Example Language icon is "dialogue by Romain J from the Noun Project."

Contents

How to Read This Book

If you want to read this book from start to finish, by all means do so; that is the best way to make sure you get all of the information. However, it is certainly not the only viable method. I designed the chapters and the sections within them to stand somewhat alone, so if you are looking for information on a specific topic or situation you can jump directly to the most relevant part. The content overlaps a great deal, though, and you will often find notes suggesting that you refer to somewhere else in the book for more information on a subject. This is to save time and avoid redundancy. For example, pronouns are relevant to almost every section, so it made the most sense to do a single detailed chapter on them and point back to it as needed. If you do read straight through, you will find that the most widely applicable chapters are at the beginning, with narrower focus near the end.

The information in this book is written from a U.S. perspective, so some of the specifics will not apply to other locations.

SECTION TYPES

Personal Experience

The whole book is in first person, but Personal Experience sections specifically describe instances from my own life. In many cases, I do not know exactly what a realistic solution would look like (for example, I have never organized a library conference and so cannot speak to the limitations involved), so I want to make it clear when I am sharing my experience rather than offering advice. Often, people with the ability to prevent transnegative situations are simply unaware that they are happening; my intention is to change some of that. I also want to highlight positive experiences, as it is very valuable to see what has worked well in practice.

Community Voices

Each Community Voices section is a contribution from another trans or gender variant library worker. I was not comfortable attempting to represent the entire community, or even letting that be implied by failing to include others' experiences. I requested short pieces on any subject that people wanted to write about as long as it related to gender identity and libraries. It was very important to me that these additional voices not be filtered through my own experiences and biases, so all of the contributions were accepted without revision. As I wanted everything in this book to come from a trans and gender variant perspective, none of these come from cisgender people.

Quick Fixes

These are concrete actions that can be accomplished relatively easily over days or weeks. Adapt whichever of these fit with your work and combine them with long-term solutions.

Long-Term Solutions

These are also concrete actions, but they may take months or years to implement successfully. Pick whichever ones make sense for you and incorporate them into long-term planning.

Glossary

The glossary at the end of the book includes brief definitions of some of the words used in the book. The Terminology section of Chapter 1, "Trans 101," has more detailed explanations of some of these. There are a great many words that are used to talk about gender, so the glossary is limited to the ones used in this book.

Acknowledgments

I don't think I truly understood how much authors mean their acknowledgment sections until now. A number of people contributed to this book in very concrete ways; many more listened to me talk through things until they made sense, offered their own perspectives, and were otherwise supportive.

First, so many thanks to those who wrote about their experiences: Max G. Bowman, Char Booth, Jay L. Colbert, Paige Flanagan, Loren Klein, Ray Lockman, Puck Malamud, JJ Pionke, Devin Spencer, and Erin White. You have added enormously to the value of this book.

Thank you to those who read and offered feedback on various bits of this book: AJ Robinson, Keely O'Connell, Kodi Saylor, Nina Exner, Liz Perry-Sizemore, Jane Sandberg, and anyone else I have forgotten.

Thank you to Kalani Adolpho for talking with me about the limitations in my own views about gender. Your work is invaluable and I greatly appreciate your sharing it.

Thank you to Lisa Lee Broughman for completely ridiculous levels of support and expertise in areas that I have absolutely no knowledge of. Several sections are far more realistic because of your input.

Thank you to the nonlibrarians who offered a different perspective: Trish Norton (my mother) and Onna McKlennon.

Finally, thank you to everyone in the Gender Variant LIS Network.

Introduction

For most of my life, I could count on libraries to be spaces where I felt comfortable and safe. When I first came out as transgender, most public places came with an added level of stress and fear. Between restroom policing by security guards and misgendering at the circulation desk, libraries were no exception. When I became a library student and then a professional librarian, I found the same issues, plus additional difficulties navigating a professional environment that remains heavily gendered. The same institutions that insist everyone should feel welcome are rife with cisnormativity and transnegative practices.

After graduate school, I found myself at a college where I was the only openly trans employee (campus-wide, not just in the library). While fortunate enough to have an incredibly supportive work environment, I still felt the lack of anyone who shared my identity. This sense of isolation seems to be fairly typical among trans and gender variant library workers. It is also not even close to the worst of our workplace difficulties, which include everything from minor microaggressions to transphobia so bad we avoid coworkers or leave jobs. It has been only ten years since the Library of Congress withdrew its job offer to Diane Schroer after she came out as transgender. It is clear that libraries have a huge distance to go before we can consider them safe workplaces for people of all gender identities.

The thing is, some libraries are doing splendidly. There are places that have prominent, accessible all-gender restrooms, that maintain current collections with good representation, that provide employees and patrons with options for name and pronoun sharing, and all the rest. There are also libraries where trans and gender variant employees are driven out by hostility from coworkers or managers and where trans patrons fear harassment for using a restroom. Gender inclusion is not taught in library school, and it is rarely part of employee training. Those places that are doing well are invariably led and staffed by people who have chosen to prioritize inclusion and have the power to do it properly. Those that are problematic may have actively transphobic employees and leadership, but more often they are simply unaware of the effects of their practices.

If I have learned anything in all of my conversations with library workers, it is that the vast majority have good intentions. Some also have the training and experience to know what to do with those intentions; a few even have the power to implement that knowledge on a large scale. However, a great many of those who want to support trans and gender variant people simply do not know how. They are afraid to say the wrong thing and so end up keeping silent, or they do not know what would make a difference, or they feel powerless due to their position. Trans and gender variant employees do not automatically know best practices for gender inclusion; those who do may fear outing themselves or risking their jobs if they try to change anything, or they (rightly) do not feel that it should be their responsibility just because of their identity. Some library workers are simply completely unaware that they have trans and gender variant patrons and coworkers, so it has never occurred to them that their practices are harmful. Transphobia is certainly a factor for some, but I choose to believe that the main issue is lack of information.

As any good librarian would, I have decided to try to solve that information need. This book is designed to provide guidance to all of those library workers who want to support trans and gender variant people but are not sure how to do so. I have intentionally provided advice for people in different positions to demonstrate that everyone can make a difference. Directors can use their power to create a gender-inclusive library, but so can circulation assistants. The librarian who sits at the reference desk will use different methods than the cataloger who never sees a patron, but both roles are important. From library school professors to systems librarians to volunteers, nobody is exempt.

So if you have gotten this far, this book is probably meant for you. It is for library directors who do not know where to start, for circulation assistants who want to avoid misgendering their coworkers, for interlibrary loan staff who want to avoid outing patrons, for instruction librarians who want to support trans students. It is for trans and gender variant library workers who are tired of defending our existence to managers. It is for everyone who wants to make sure that libraries actually are for everyone.

AUTHOR'S PERSPECTIVE

I think that this book is one of the many instances when it is important for the author to acknowledge their own identity and its limitations. I am a white, abled, transmasculine person who was born and raised in the continental United States. My pronouns are he/him or they/them. Most people read me as a cisgender man based on my appearance, though I make no secret of being transgender; I am out in all aspects of my life and am fortunate enough to have been accepted and supported in most of them. All of this makes me incredibly privileged compared to a great many other trans and gender variant people. Individual experiences vary widely; I do not speak for everyone of my own identity, let alone all trans and gender variant people. This why I have written in first person throughout the book. There is danger in forgetting that all authors and scholars are individuals whose backgrounds and experiences influence their work.

This is also the reason for the Community Voices sections, which are all written by trans or gender variant library workers; I wanted to make sure that mine was not the only perspective represented. These are all presented as written, unedited by me, to ensure that multiple voices come through. For the most part, I have tried to write from my perspective as a practicing librarian. However, I am also a trans person who works in and uses libraries. The Personal Experience sections focus on my experiences from that angle; I use them to share how I felt and behaved in various situations. These are not meant to imply that all trans and gender variant people have the same experiences or reactions, though many may.

Throughout the book, I remind readers that simply being a trans or gender variant person does not mean that one automatically knows the best way to create a gender-inclusive space. I am no exception. In addition to my personal experiences and my work as a librarian, I have put a great deal of time and labor into educating myself about gender inclusion. Delightfully, there is now a large amount of published scholarship on gender identity, and I certainly do not pretend to have read more than a little of it. There is far less on trans and gender variant people in libraries and I do try to keep up with current work in that area, especially when it comes from and/or focuses on a perspective other than my own. In general, I go to every Safe Zone or similar training that I can—even if I know all of the material covered, which is certainly not always the case, I invariably learn something about how to (or how not to) share it. To someone writing about gender inclusion, this ongoing education is as important as my own gender identity and work experience.

HOW TO USE THIS BOOK

This book is designed to provide practical guidelines for creating a library where people of all genders feel comfortable. It is not designed to tell you how gender identity works or provide detailed information on the many, many different genders that exist. Chapter 1, "Trans 101," is there to supply the minimal amount of information that you must have in order to begin understanding why gender inclusion work is important. Please do not finish this book and conclude that you now understand gender identity; that requires a great deal more work on your part, which I strongly encourage you to do. Also, do not finish this book, do everything recommended in it, and assume that your job is done and your library is now safe for all trans and gender variant people. An essential part of gender inclusion work is that you and your workplace keep learning and growing.

This book is not intended to tell anyone exactly what will work in their situation. Take the information here and adapt it to your needs. Perhaps your patrons include a group that uses specific terminology for gender; take the time to learn it rather than parroting the example language that I suggest. Talk to your employees and coworkers to determine what a realistic version of gender-inclusive practices looks like in your library. Remember that the way we view gender changes over time, so keep your approach adaptable and update it regularly, always using current resources (I hope that a lot of this book remains useful for some time, but I am certain that some of the specifics in it will be obsolete within a few years or less.) Think about the information in this book as a starting point, intended to help you understand why gender inclusion is important and to demonstrate examples. It is your responsibility to assess your own library and determine what will work best there.

Trans and gender variant people are certainly not the only ones for whom libraries can be unwelcoming. It is possible that some of the information here can be adapted to support other marginalized groups, as there is often some overlap in the general aspects of equity, diversity, and inclusion. However, I am writing specifically from a trans perspective, and nothing in this book should be assumed to apply to any other identity. I do strongly encourage you to do the same type of intentional inclusion work for people of color, people with disabilities, non-Christian people, and others who have historically been excluded by libraries in the United States. Find resources by and about the people that you want to support; then commit time, labor, and funding to improving. Some trans and gender variant people face additional challenges because they fall into one or more other marginalized groups. This means that gender inclusion is inseparable from other types of equity work. Intersecting identities must be recognized and supported; otherwise, gender inclusion is synonymous with ableism and white supremacy.

Will it be difficult to create a gender-inclusive society, even a contained one like a single library? Yes, probably. It involves ongoing active work and no small amount of awkwardness as people struggle with their internalized assumptions and biases about gender. Some people will actively resist; others will not see the purpose and fail to participate. You may feel alone and ineffective. If you are trans or gender variant, please take care of yourself first, as the emotional toll of bringing your own identity into your work is considerable. If you are cisgender, imagine how much more difficult this labor is for those who are not. The more people who participate in gender inclusion work, the easier it becomes for the people doing it as well as those affected by it. If you are not personally affected by anything in this book, use that privilege to help those who are.

As established, I do not speak for all trans and gender variant people. For my part, I notice every time someone engages in gender inclusion work. I relax a little whenever a building has an all-gender restroom. I feel a little safer every time someone else shares their pronouns. I feel more comfortable applying for jobs when gender identity and expression are explicitly listed in the nondiscrimination statement. I am pleasantly surprised when a form lets me fill in my own gender. I promise that even (especially) with the seemingly small things, even if nobody ever mentions it, this work makes a difference.

1

Trans 101

This chapter will provide some context for the rest of the book. I will not attempt to comprehensively explain how gender works or what it means to be trans or gender variant; that would take an enormous amount of time and I want to move on to library practices. Instead, I am going to highlight a few different types of information that will help you make sense of the following chapters. In this chapter you will find definitions for the terms used throughout the book, some common behavior mistakes and what to do instead, and a discussion on the importance of knowing one's community. Please bear in mind that this chapter contains a very small amount of information on a very large topic; please do not mistake it for everything there is to know about gender. Also remember that the way we view gender changes over time and varies between individuals and groups. This material may not apply to everyone even now, and some or all of it will become outdated eventually.

ABOUT GENDER IDENTITY

Everyone has a gender identity. This is your personal sense of gender; it may be male, female, neither, both, somewhere in between, or something else entirely. For trans and gender variant people, this identity differs in some way from the sex assigned at birth. I was assigned female at birth (AFAB) and now I am male. This is one of many, many different types of trans identity. Many people, whatever their original assigned sex, are not strictly male or female. People can be genderqueer, transmasculine, female, nonbinary, genderfluid, agender, male, transfeminine, and more. Some people identify with multiple different terms simultaneously. There are genders tied to specific groups or cultures, such as *fa'afafine*, *hijra*, and *muxe*.

The language we use for gender varies widely between groups; factors include location, culture, age, identity, and others. Some words may be the norm in one group but completely unused by another, even for seemingly similar identities. Language also changes over time. There are terms that were widely used twenty years ago that many people now consider outdated or offensive, but that some people still identify with. There is no universal rule for what language is appropriate; the best approach is to accept whatever terms people have used for themselves without assuming that these apply to others. Self-identification is the most important element when talking about gender identity. Another aspect of this is that individuals may change how they identify and/or what language they use over their lives. Part of respecting self-identification is supporting someone when they ask you to use new language for them.

Trans and gender variant people live and express our genders in many different ways. We can share our pronouns, legally change our name and gender, and undergo hormone therapy and surgery; we can also do one or some or none of these things. We can wear whatever we choose; we can come out to friends or everyone we meet or nobody at all. We can be any sexual or romantic orientation, as those things are completely different from gender identity. We can present and behave a certain way in one setting and completely differently in another; we can also change any of this from one day to the next. This is the case whether we are nonbinary, genderfluid, male, female, or anything else. In an ideal world, we would make all of these decisions based on our own preference; however, many people are limited by (often justified) fear, cost barriers, social stigma, lack of knowledge or support, or self-preservation. Trans and gender variant people should be able to look, sound, act, and live in any way without undermining our gender identity, as should cisgender people.

The point of all this is that you cannot know someone's gender identity unless they tell you. Nor do you need to know: the only information you need to respectfully interact with someone is what they want you to call them (that is, name, pronouns, and possibly title or honorific). Their gender identity, legal gender, physical body, and legal name are none of your business unless they volunteer that information. Whatever your own identity, start your gender inclusion work by thinking about your assumptions and biases. Everyone has these (mine still catch me off guard sometimes); acknowledging and dismantling them is an ongoing and essential part of supporting all trans and gender variant people.

TERMINOLOGY

There are a great many terms that we use to describe gender, and I am not going to attempt to cover all of them here. That said, I do want to define the terms that appear most often in this book. The definitions are not absolute, and some people may not use exactly the same ones, but this is what I mean when I use these words. For quick reference, there is a glossary at the end of the book with brief versions of these definitions. If you want a more comprehensive list of other terms, I recommend the Trans Language Primer (www.translanguageprimer.org), which is extensive, regularly updated, and written by trans and gender variant people.

Allyship: Behavior that supports a marginalized group (in this case, trans and gender variant people). One becomes a trans ally by actively and consistently engaging in such behavior. Simply declaring that you are an ally is meaningless on its own; allyship is an ongoing series of actions, not a state of being.

Cisgender: Adjective describing people whose gender matches the sex assigned to them at birth. Often abbreviated to *cis*.

Cisnormative: Treating cisgender people as the norm and all others as anomalous (or failing to acknowledge the existence of trans and gender variant people entirely).

Coming out: When an LGBTQ+ person tells someone about that part of their identity. This can be anything from one-on-one conversation to a public social media post. Coming out to one person or group does not mean that someone is out to everyone.

Gender binary: The false idea that everyone is either exclusively male or exclusively female. In actuality, many people are somewhere in between, a combination of both, or neither at all.

Gender identity: One's personal sense of being nonbinary, female, agender, genderqueer, male, genderfluid, or any number of other things. Everyone has a gender identity, and it does not always match one's legal gender.

Legal gender: The marker listed on one's driver's license and other documentation. For many trans and gender variant people, this does not match their gender identity. The process for changing it varies from state to state. Several have introduced a gender-neutral option in addition to the male and female designations, but this is not yet widespread in the United States as of the writing of this book.

Legal name: The name that is on a person's documentation (driver's license, Social Security card, bank account, etc.). In the United States, the process for changing one's legal name varies from state to state; it usually takes significant quantities of time and money, so not everyone is able to do it even if they want to. When speaking to or about someone, always refer to them by their name of use instead of their legal name.

LGBTQ+: Umbrella adjective for all people that are not cisgender or heterosexual. Includes lesbian, gay, bisexual, transgender, queer, asexual, intersex, and others. (My personal preferred umbrella term for this is "queer," but not everyone agrees on that. Some people find the word offensive due to its history as a slur, though an active reclamation movement means that many people self-identify with it.)

Misgender: To assign gender to someone incorrectly. This includes using the wrong pronouns, describing a person with gendered language that does not apply to them (e.g., calling a nonbinary person a woman), and telling someone to do something based on your incorrect assumption about their gender (such as which restroom to use).

Name of use: The name that a person wants others to call them. For many trans and gender variant people, as well as cis people who go by a nickname or middle name, the name of use differs from the legal name. Synonymous with *preferred name*, but I do not like the implication that using someone's correct name is preferred or optional. Calling someone by anything but their name of use is incredibly rude.

Nonbinary: Adjective describing people who do not identify as male or female. Sometimes this is used as an umbrella term intended to include a variety of identities; sometimes it refers to a specific person's identity. As always, listen to individuals who tell you what language to use or to avoid; for example, one genderqueer person might consider themselves to be nonbinary, while another might not.

Outing: Disclosing someone's gender or other LGBTQ+ identity without their consent. This can be accidental or intentional. Do not do it.

Trans and gender variant: Adjective describing people who do not fully identify with the gender assigned to them at birth. I use this term to include transgender, nonbinary, genderqueer, and genderfluid people, among others; however, it is up to individuals to choose what terms accurately describe them.

Transnegative: Contributing to a negative experience for trans and gender variant people. I use this term because *transphobic* focuses on the feelings of the individual rather than the results of their actions. One does not have to hate or disrespect trans and gender variant people to participate in their oppression, often inadvertently. The history of erasure and oppression of trans and gender variant people means that many practices that we consider normal are transnegative, even if individuals do not intend to make them so.

COMMON TRANSNEGATIVE BEHAVIORS

There are some extremely common behaviors that often make trans and gender variant people feel uncomfortable or unsafe. They may manifest in any number of different ways; some of the specific ones are covered in relevant chapters throughout the book, but this section will identify and explain the general problems as well as offer solutions. The exception to anything that follows is if you have talked to an individual and have their explicit consent to do something different, in which case you should do as they ask (do not assume that anyone else feels the same, though).

Do not assume gender. If you remember one thing from this book, it should be that you cannot tell a person's gender unless they tell you. I will say it again: *You do not know someone's gender unless they tell you.* Trans and gender variant people present in all sorts of ways; for that matter, so do cis people. Someone's clothing, makeup, physical shape, name, or voice does not mean that they are nonbinary, male, female, or any other gender. Some women, cisgender as well as trans and gender variant, wear suits and have short hair. Some men, trans or otherwise, wear eyeliner. Traditionally gendered names may belong to men, women, or people who are neither. Nonbinary people may present in all sorts of ways, some of them seemingly identical to a male or female person. The social, financial, and other barriers to physical transition mean that many trans and gender variant people cannot fully present the way they want to; others may simply choose not to undergo procedures like hormone replacement therapy or surgery. None of this undermines a person's gender or their right to be treated with respect. Cisgender and binary norms are so pervasive in many societies that it may take a lot of work to break the habit of assuming gender.

Do assess your own thoughts and biases. Do you expect women to look a certain way and men another? Do you automatically assign pronouns based on those expectations? Practice using neutral pronouns whenever you have not been told which ones to use for someone. Try to notice when you assume gender without realizing it, such as when someone asks for directions to the restroom. Undoing years of habit takes time and labor, but it is an integral part of allyship and basic human decency.

Do not perpetuate the gender binary. Some trans and gender variant people do identify as male or female, but many have other genders. If your version of inclusion accepts only trans men and trans women, it is not inclusion at all. Do not question the validity of nonbinary, genderqueer, agender, genderfluid, and other identities that do not fit into the gender binary; never suggest that they are a temporary, undecided, or in-between step for someone who will eventually become male or female.

Do acknowledge all genders. Gender inclusion means respecting all genders, not just male and female. Correctly using the pronouns of a nonbinary person is as important as doing the same for a trans man or trans woman. People who do not fall within the gender binary deserve just as much respect as those who do.

Do not out people. Outing, in the context of this book, means telling a person someone else's gender without permission. At best, it is rude to share that kind of personal information; it should be up to the individual whom they tell and how. In many cases, outing someone can also be harmful or dangerous. Perhaps they will lose financial support from parents, or be fired from a job, or be physically attacked if their identity becomes known. Perhaps they simply want to come out at their own pace. Perhaps they prefer never to come out at all. Many trans and gender variant people are out in different ways depending on the context; someone may use one name socially but another at work, or be out to friends but not to family.

Do trust that the person is doing what is safest and most comfortable for them. If someone comes out to you, it never hurts to check about who else they have told and whether they want you to share the information or not.

In some cases, sharing the information may be helpful. For example, an employee might come out to a manager and ask them to tell other employees so that they do not have to have multiple conversations. Some people may be out in all aspects of their life and have no problem with other people knowing their gender. However, you should always check before telling others that someone is trans or gender variant.

Do not ask someone's legal name. Apart from some exceptions (billing, background checks, etc.), there is no reason that anyone needs to know another person's past or current legal name. Name of use should be the default for all interactions and communications. Demanding to know a different one implies that you do not think that their identity is valid, especially when explicitly phrased as such (e.g., "No, your *real* name"). For many trans and gender variant people, the legal name is a source of discomfort, pain, or trauma.

Do be clear about how names are used. If you do need to know someone's legal name for a work-related reason, ask them privately and tell them why. Also let them know exactly who will see the information, and make sure that anyone who does see the legal name knows the name of use as well. If you happen to learn someone's legal name and it differs from their name of use, never call them by it or share it with anyone else unless they have explicitly asked you to.

Do not ask someone about their gender identity or legal gender. The only information you need for day-to-day interaction with someone is how they want you to refer to them (that is, their name of use and pronouns). You do not need to know their gender, whether they are trans or gender variant, or anything else. You especially do not need to know their legal gender, which can be difficult (or, for nonbinary people in many places, impossible) to change even if one wants to. It is fine to talk about any of this if someone chooses to share that information with you, but do not ask unless they bring it up.

Do share your own pronouns. The simplest way to invite someone to tell you their pronouns is to share your own. If this is a new concept, take the time to practice and become comfortable with it. There are a variety of reasons why a person might not want to share their pronouns; you are certainly not obligated to do so if this is the case for you, and you should not expect it from anyone else. See Chapter 2, "Pronouns and Other Language," for more information on pronoun sharing.

Do not ask someone about their body or physical transition. It is extraordinarily rude to ask anyone about their genitalia, whatever their gender. Also, do not ask about hormone therapy, top and bottom surgery, or anything else about someone's physical transition, including whether or not they plan to do any of these things. Even if it is someone you know well, and even if they have talked about their body before, they may not always want to do so. Never ask simply out of curiosity, especially if you do not know the person well. Trans and gender variant people are not there to entertain or educate you, and there is plenty of publicly available information by people willing to share their own experiences. Look for books, blogs, vlogs, and other resources that are created by trans and gender variant people.

Do think before you speak. Consider whether you would say the same thing to a cisgender person. Also remember that talking about our bodies and transition can be incredibly difficult and traumatic. If talking to someone you know who seems willing to share their experiences, always ask if they are comfortable talking about this with you, and provide an easy way for them to opt out of the conversation.

Do not assume that silence is neutral. For the most part, U.S. society is overwhelmingly cisnormative, and libraries are no exception. Failure to acknowledge this results in continued transnegativity. If you are not actively assessing existing practices in your library to see if they perpetuate the gender binary and cisgender privilege, then you are continuing the oppression that trans and gender variant people face constantly.

Do take action to create equitable norms. It is very important to normalize gender-inclusive practices so that trans and gender variant people can easily exist and interact with others. Because of the aforementioned cisnormativity, this takes active work by everyone. The information in this book should help you engage in that work.

Do not imagine that cisgender equals neutral, or that cis people are inherently unqualified for gender inclusion work. The nature of cisnormativity is that only trans and gender variant people end up sharing our gender identities and pronouns; it does not occur to some cis people that they, too, have these things. Some cis people also feel uncomfortable leading or even participating in gender inclusion initiatives. There is no reason for this; everyone can and should make it part of their work, and active allyship is desperately needed.

Do acknowledge the values and limitations of your own perspective. When doing gender inclusion work, especially when writing, presenting, or otherwise spreading information to others, be clear about your own identity if you are comfortable doing so. Cisgender people should not feel automatically unqualified for this work because they are not trans or gender variant. However, they should make it clear that they are coming from a position of cisgender privilege. This does not make anything they say less valid; it merely acknowledges that they do not speak from personal experience the way a trans or gender variant person might. (Side note: It is worthwhile to explore the pressures that a cisnormative and binarist society puts on all people, such as shaming women who do not shave their armpits, pressuring parents to give children gendered toys, and judging men who engage in "feminine" hobbies. None of these are comparable to the difficulties that trans and gender variant people face in order to exist, and they in no way outweigh cisgender privilege, but the gender binary is harmful for everyone and that should be acknowledged.) It is not unusual for cisgender people with trans and gender variant family or friends to become involved in gender inclusion work. If this is the case, remember that you still cannot speak directly for them or for other trans and gender variant people. Whatever your perspective, clearly sharing it allows your audience to understand where you are coming from and to respond accordingly.

Do not expect trans and gender variant people to do the labor. Trans and gender variant people often end up leading gender inclusion work out of desperation and self-defense. These are terrible reasons to feel forced to take on a task, especially in a workplace. Do not expect individual trans and gender variant people to do the work unless it is explicitly part of their job description or they have otherwise expressed interest. Do not ask trans and gender variant people for their time and energy just so you can mark a diversity checkbox or because you do not want or know how to take on the labor yourself.

Do take responsibility for the work. It is the responsibility of everyone to dismantle the transnegativity around them. If you are not sure where to start, consult established resources for help.

Personal Experience

I have noticed two different tones when someone asks me to do gender inclusion work. At my institution, this is not part of my official job description; however, I do have several roles (member of a relevant committee, adviser of the LGBTQ+ group) that incorporate it. Because I volunteered for those roles, I have no objection to doing something like researching Safe Zone options as part of them. My identity may give me a useful perspective, but it is not the reason that I was asked to do the work, or at least not the primary one. Similarly, I have presented and led workshops on the type of information covered in this book; I can do this from the perspective of a trans person, but I volunteer or am invited because of my published research on gender inclusion. When someone asks me to do gender inclusion work with no reference to a chosen role or to my research, however, I feel tokenized and used for my identity. There is an enormous difference between being asked because of my work and asked because I am openly trans and someone wanted to check a diversity box.

When asking a trans or gender variant person to do gender inclusion work, think about why you are going to them. Is this part of their job and/or scholarly work? Have they invited people to come to them about this topic? Do you want to learn how to participate in the work yourself? If the answer to all of these questions is not yes, look for other options. Simply being trans or gender variant does not make someone qualified to do, let alone lead, gender inclusion work. This labor also can be especially stressful for trans and gender variant people because it involves our own identities.

Do not assign language to individuals or groups. Language for gender varies widely between groups and individuals; it has also changed over time and continues to do so. One result of this variability is that some people may identify with words that others find inapplicable or offensive. Do not assume that any given term applies to an individual or group unless they have explicitly told you so. Also do not tell anyone that the language they use for themselves is wrong, as this is impossible. There are any number of reasons why someone might identify with one term over another. It is not your business why a person uses certain language to describe themselves; nobody should have to defend or explain their self-identification to anyone else. Whatever your own identity, respect the language that others use for themselves (this goes for other trans and gender variant as well as cisgender people). Some people take time to explore their own identities, so do not express frustration to or shame anyone who describes themselves in one way and later switches to different language.

Do support self-identification. If someone tells you how they identify, respect that and use that language for them. For example, I am a queer trans man, and I would be offended if someone described me as transsexual. You might meet someone who seems to have a similar identity who calls themselves transsexual and dislikes the word queer. Simply describe each of us using the language we chose. Recognize that individuals may change their self-identification over their lives, either because they are exploring different ways of existing or because they are learning new language that may fit them better than the old (or both).

Personal Experience

I referred to myself as a lesbian for years before I decided that queer suited me better, and I would almost certainly have identified as nonbinary at some point if I had known the language for it. FTM (female to male) was an important term for me when I first heard it because it described me better than anything I had previously found; I later learned the term AFAB (assigned female at birth), which is a more accurate descriptor for my experience, so I started using that instead.

Trans and gender variant people may use different names, pronouns, and terminology as we change over time or learn new ways of describing ourselves. Respecting that is an important element of allyship; always put effort into referring to people as they request.

Do not be afraid to make mistakes. Normalizing gender-inclusive habits takes time, for individuals as well as institutions. Practice is the best way to improve, and mistakes are inevitable. It makes sense to fear doing or saying something wrong, but doing nothing is ultimately worse. If you do catch yourself, do not dwell on the error, as this centers your own experience and makes it more difficult to progress. It can also be awkward for the people you are trying to support. For example, many trans and gender variant people are misgendered often enough that drawing extended attention to each instance takes an untenable amount of emotional energy and detracts from meaningful interactions.

Do learn from your mistakes. As long as you are making an effort to improve, errors are fine. Most people are aware that they are part of the process and will not judge you for them. For small mistakes, simply apologize briefly, correct yourself, move on, and take steps on your own time to improve. Cisnormativity is something that everyone has to work to overcome, so do not feel guilty when it takes you time and practice. Mistakes will happen less and less over time, and eventually gender-inclusive habits will come naturally.

LEARN YOUR COMMUNITY

The experiences of trans and gender variant people vary widely, even among those of similar identities. Age, race, economic status, religion, disability, and other factors can all contribute to the degree of marginalization faced by a trans or gender variant person. For example, the 2015 U.S. Transgender Survey reported that 26 percent of its Black nonbinary respondents were unemployed, compared to 20 percent of all Black respondents and 15 percent overall (James, Brown, and Wilson, 2017, p. 8). The survey also reported that 45 percent of respondents with disabilities were living in poverty, which was the case for 30 percent of all respondents and 12 percent of the total U.S. population (James et al., 2016, p. 6). The vast majority of trans people killed in the United States are trans women of color (Lee, 2017, p. 34). I cite these numbers to demonstrate that trans and gender variant people can face increased difficulties if they also belong to other marginalized groups. As you read through this book, consider how other factors may affect the trans and gender variant people you are trying to support. Are your all-gender restrooms wheelchair-accessible? If not, a trans or gender variant person who uses a wheelchair and one who does not are not receiving equitable treatment. If your system uses patrons' legal names, those without the financial resources for a name change cannot go by the name they want to in the library, while others can. Do not only consider the needs of white, abled, middle-class, binary trans people, but do the work to ensure that all trans and gender variant people receive the same kind of support.

The language that I use in this book was developed in the Westernized colonialist society that I am a part of. Among other things, this means that it does not accurately describe all people, especially those who come from outside of that cultural context. Many indigenous groups have people that may not consider themselves transgender or cisgender, however one defines those terms. I use "trans and gender variant" as an umbrella term in an attempt to acknowledge these identities, but this is by no means a perfect or all-inclusive way to do so. When working to support people of all gender identities, remember that the language you use comes with its own connotations and biases. If someone asks you to use something different to describe them, respect their wishes. Do not be afraid to recognize your own biases when they are pointed out; it is the first step to dismantling them. Kalani Adolpho points out these and other limitations in Western definitions of gender in a library context (Adolpho, 2018).

This section has barely touched on some of the complexities and limitations of gender inclusion work, and I am by no means an expert on all of them. What I want you to remember is that trans and gender variant people come from all backgrounds, and our experiences vary as widely as those of cisgender people. This book is not intended as a substitute for learning the specific needs of your community. Part of the reason that I am not defining every term and conjugating every pronoun is that I would inevitably leave someone out. Another part is that different people use the same terms in different ways, and I do not want to provide you with a definition when the people you work with use another one. It is your responsibility to learn the particulars of the people you serve. This includes general awareness of the different experiences trans and gender variant people have so that you can better support library patrons and employees on an individual basis. If you work in a specialized space such as a school or a prison, educate yourself about the specific needs of trans and gender variant people within that environment. If you work in a tribal library or otherwise have a large local population that might have specific ways of viewing gender, learn about it instead of trying to apply outside language and assumptions. Try reaching out to professional organizations and listservs or local LGBTQ+ groups if you are not sure where to start with your community, location, or library type.

In addition to familiarizing yourself with the perspectives of your trans and gender variant patrons, consider the local external factors that affect them. Does your state have laws regulating who can use which restrooms? Take special care to develop a public gender-inclusive restroom policy, and educate your employees about how to apply it and respond to challenges. Is it particularly difficult to get a name change there? Even more than usual, train the circulation staff to ask for name of use when making library cards. Are there state workplace protections for LGBTQ+ people? If not, make sure your library has a nondiscrimination statement for employees that explicitly covers gender identity, gender expression, and genetic information; append this statement to all job postings. All of this should be general practice everywhere, but some things may be more relevant in one place than another.

The information in this book can be adapted to fit many different environments, but how to best apply it may vary. If trans or gender variant employees or patrons tell you that something does not work for them, listen and be open to other approaches. The purpose of everything suggested here is to create an environment in your library where trans and gender variant people feel welcome. This may not mean making sweeping changes; it may simply be demonstrating that you are prioritizing that goal and are open to feedback. Even if you perfectly understand the needs of your local community now, they will change over time, so the best way to create a long-term gender-inclusive environment is to establish open communication with the people you want to serve.

REFERENCES

Adolpho, Kalani. *Gender Diversity and Transgender Inclusivity in Libraries.* Presentation, Joint Conference of Librarians of Color, Albuquerque, NM, September 2018. https://drive.google.com/file/d/1R6UbIjoff0RjjXkBHKBbGRikbMvawGnt /view (accessed May 7, 2019).

James, Sandy E., Carter Brown, and Isaiah Wilson. *2015 U.S. Transgender Survey: Report on the Experiences of Black Respondents.* Washington, DC and Dallas, TX: National Center for Transgender Equality, Black Trans Advocacy, and National Black Justice Coalition, 2017. http://www.transequality.org/sites/default/files/docs/ usts/USTSBlackRespondentsReport-Nov17.pdf (accessed May 7, 2019).

James, Sandy E., Jody L. Herman, Susan Rankin, Mara Keisling, Lisa Mottet, and Ma'ayan Anafi. *The Report of the 2015 U.S. Transgender Survey.* Washington, DC: National Center for Transgender Equality, 2016. https://transequality.org/ sites/default/files/docs/usts/USTS-Full-Report-Dec17.pdf (accessed May 7, 2019).

Lee, Mark. *A Time to Act: Fatal Violence Against Trans People in America in 2017.* Human Rights Campaign Foundation and Trans People of Color Coalition, 2017. http://assets2.hrc.org/files/assets/resources/A_Time_To_Act_2017_REV3.pdf (accessed May 7, 2019).

2

Pronouns and Other Language

A note on scope: I am a native English speaker; while I have some knowledge of other languages, I am not fluent in any. The information in this chapter is wholly based on American English and is not intended to apply to other languages, many of which have very different ways of describing gender.

WHAT ARE PERSONAL PRONOUNS?

Personal pronouns are the words used to refer to an individual in place of their name or another identifier. Everyone has personal pronouns. For example, if you are a cisgender woman (that is, you were assigned female at birth and identify as female), you probably use *she/her* pronouns for yourself. Trans and gender variant people may use different sets of pronouns at different times in our lives. Often, pronouns are assumed to correspond with a particular gender (for example, someone using *she/her* pronouns is assumed to be female), but this is incorrect. When a person tells you what pronouns to use for them, all that means is that this is how you should refer to them. It does not mean that they are male, female, nonbinary, transgender, or anything else except how to respectfully describe them. Some people may go by multiple sets of pronouns (for example, my pronouns are *he/him* or *they/them*, which means that people can call me by either of those).

In the English language, pronouns are one of the most pervasive everyday ways in which gender identities are affirmed or dismissed, sometimes unintentionally. One important way to support trans and gender variant people day-to-day is to learn people's pronouns and use them correctly, including sharing your own. This is something that everyone can start doing immediately. It will probably feel awkward at first, but the only barrier to inclusive pronoun use is the time and effort needed to make it come naturally.

> **EXAMPLE LANGUAGE**
>
> *Examples of Personal Pronouns*
>
> They/them/their/theirs/themself
>
> He/him/his/himself
>
> Zie/zim/zir/zirself
>
> She/her/hers/herself
>
> Name (Stephen/Stephen's/Stephen's self)
>
> Initial (S/S's/S's self)
>
> Ve/ver/vis/vers/verself

On Gender-Neutral Pronouns

Some of the pronouns in the Example Language sidebar are gender-neutral; *they/them/their/theirs/themself* is probably the most widely used. I have not attempted to enumerate all of the different pronouns here because I will inevitably miss some, and I do not want readers to treat this as an authoritative list. New pronouns come into use over time, so any such list would be incomplete and obsolete anyway. Do not obsess over memorizing all of the different options. Instead, develop the habit of learning and using the pronouns of everyone you interact with. You may have a patron or coworker who uses ones that you have never heard before, but it is no less important that you use them respectfully.

You may hear, or be tempted to suggest yourself, that it is grammatically incorrect to use *they/them* pronouns for an individual, as those pronouns are plural. For one thing, this is entirely wrong: Merriam-Webster and the Oxford English Dictionary both point to the use of *they* as a singular pronoun starting in the 1300s and growing increasingly common since (Merriam-Webster, 2018; Oxford University Press, 2018). Even were this not the case, it is unacceptable to prioritize habitual language use over respecting a person's identity.

They/them pronouns are used by some nonbinary individuals as their main personal pronouns, but that is not the only situation in which they are appropriate. Use *they/them* when describing an individual whose pronouns you do not know or whose gender you do not want to disclose. Always use *they/them* in situations such as job postings, when the candidate might be of any gender (this is both more inclusive and less clunky than writing out *s/he* or *him or her*). Unless someone has told you their pronouns, it is perfectly acceptable to default to *they/them* for any individual. This is only misgendering if the person has requested that you use something else and you fail to do so.

Multiple Pronouns

People can go by multiple sets of pronouns for a variety of reasons. Some cisgender and binary trans people list *they/them* when they share their pronouns ("my pronouns are he/him or they/them"). I fully support this practice, as it normalizes singular gender-neutral pronouns. Some trans and gender variant people go by different pronouns in different contexts, or they are trying several to see what fits them best, or they truly do not care what pronouns are used for them, or they express their gender by using multiple different pronouns. You do not need to know anyone's reasons; simply call them whatever they ask to be called. If someone lists multiple pronouns and you are unsure what to call them, it is fine to just use the first ones listed, but trust that they would not have included any that they were uncomfortable with. If someone says that they do not care but does not list any options, default to *they/them*.

MISGENDERING

Correctly using people's pronouns is one of the simplest ways to show respect. It is such a basic behavior that it should not even be worth noting. For many people, however, this cannot be counted on. *Misgendering* happens when someone incorrectly assumes or describes the gender of another person. In English, this most often happens through incorrect use of name and pronouns. In my case, someone might misgender me by using the name that I was given at birth, calling me *she*, or describing me as a woman. Note that this is not an issue only for trans and gender variant people. A cisgender woman who wears her hair short and dresses in a suit may have people call her *him*; this is also misgendering because it is assigning gendered language to someone incorrectly. Group language, such as *men* or *girls*, misgenders anyone in the group who does not fit that description; phrasing like *ladies and gentlemen* misgenders any nonbinary people present by implicitly assigning them to one of the two groups listed.

Intentional and Accidental Misgendering

There is a huge difference between intentional and accidental misgendering. Intentional misgendering happens when someone insists on using one set of pronouns or other gendered language for a person who they know identifies differently. For example, repeatedly using *he/him* pronouns for a trans woman, insisting that she use the men's restroom, or calling her a man, even after being corrected, is intentional misgendering. This is, at best, extraordinarily disrespectful; some have called it an act of violence (Ford, 2014), and I do not disagree. Rejecting someone's gender identity dehumanizes them and lets them know that you are not someone they can feel safe around. It can harm your relationship with them, their self-esteem, and their ability to feel comfortable in any space where they might see you. If it goes beyond language—policing restroom use, for example—it can also cause them physical harm if you out them or force them into a situation where other people react badly. Intentional misgendering is never acceptable.

Accidental misgendering is an entirely different issue. It is still not acceptable to consistently misgender anyone, but mistakes do happen. Perhaps you know someone who transitioned and you occasionally use their old pronouns out of habit; perhaps you are learning a new set of neutral pronouns and need time and practice before they come naturally. It is up to you to do the work of learning, but most people will understand if you are clearly making an effort to improve. Even if it starts out unintentionally, repeated misgendering without any effort to stop is indiscernible from the intentional form described above, which is unacceptable and harmful. See below to learn what to do if you accidentally misgender someone.

Consequences in the Library

Misgendering people is obviously unacceptable for reasons of courtesy and basic human decency. In the context of library work, it also has a number of practical repercussions. Patrons who are misgendered by library employees may not feel comfortable using the library; they may even stop doing so entirely and spread the word that the space is not trans-friendly. Most libraries put a lot of work into getting people in the door, and this clearly counters those efforts in a tangible way. It also directly conflicts with any rhetoric claiming that libraries are for everyone and that people of all backgrounds and identities are welcome. This language is common in the library profession; less common is the sincere work needed to make it true. Avoiding misgendering must be part of that work, and it should be incorporated into both individual behavior and institutional policy.

Trans and gender variant library employees are often subject to misgendering by colleagues and patrons alike. If intentional or uncorrected, this creates an extremely toxic work environment. Relationships with coworkers and patrons will suffer, affecting any work activities that depend on those relationships. Feeling disrespected or unsafe makes it extremely difficult to do one's best, understandably, so the quality of work may suffer. If someone appeals to a manager or other resource for help and does not receive support, that relationship may also suffer. Coworkers and patrons who are not personally affected will nevertheless see library employees being treated disrespectfully, which may affect how they view the person doing the misgendering as well as the library as a space that permits it.

It is not the duty of any trans or gender variant person to educate the people around them in order to feel safe, though this often does happen out of self-defense or frustration. Everyone is responsible for how they interact with their colleagues, which includes educating oneself on how to treat people with respect. In addition, those with the power to do so (such as managers, supervisors, and directors) can institute workplace policies that minimize misgendering, by patrons as well as employees. Some specific ideas on that are outlined below.

PRACTICING PRONOUNS

It may take time before some pronouns sound natural to you. That is okay! It takes practice to learn any unfamiliar terms, and singular gender-neutral pronouns are new for a lot of people. This does not, however, mean that you have an excuse not to use them. Most trans and gender variant people are well aware that it takes time and practice to adjust to new pronouns, so you will not be resented for making mistakes as long as it is clear that you are making the effort to improve.

If you are having trouble learning a new set of pronouns, find ways to practice where you will not hurt anyone or feel guilty for slipping up. The *Trans Allyship Workbook* suggests assigning different pronouns to everyday objects, such as kitchen tools, to give yourself a low-stakes way to practice (Shlasko, 2017). This is good both for learning unfamiliar language and for practicing changing how you refer to someone. I use *they/them* pronouns for my cats and Dungeons & Dragons characters; this gives me space to practice without hurting a real live human by misgendering them.

Personal Experience

I now know a great many people who use gender-neutral pronouns, but for years I did not know that nonbinary people existed at all. It took me some time to grow accustomed to unfamiliar pronoun sets. I remember, very clearly and with great shame, making the argument that *they* as a singular pronoun was grammatically incorrect (this obviously now makes me cringe). My point here is that I know exactly how difficult it can be to learn a new way of using language. Perhaps you have never had a person ask you to use neutral pronouns (note that this does not mean that you do not know anyone who does, just that they have not come out to you); perhaps you have not noticed them in your reading or other media. My own use of language is heavily based on the books I read as a child and a teenager, and I do not remember a single nonbinary person in any of them (I dearly wish that I had been exposed to LGBTQ+ literature earlier than I was, but we will get to that in Chapter 12, "Collection Development"). It has taken time and practice to retrain my spoken, written, and mental reflexes, and it will most likely take the same for you.

SHARING PRONOUNS

Sharing pronouns is when you tell other people what pronouns you want them to use for you. This may be part of a verbal introduction; it can also be part of a nametag, email signature, social media bio, or other written form. The goals of pronoun sharing are twofold. First, sharing your pronouns helps people avoid misgendering you and implicitly invites others to share their own. Second, it normalizes the practice, which means that trans and gender variant people do not have to automatically out themselves by being the only ones to share our pronouns. This is why I strongly encourage everyone who is comfortable doing so to adopt the practices below. Do this even (or especially) if you are cisgender and/or if people generally assign the correct pronouns to you.

The exception is that nobody of any gender identity who feels uncomfortable about it should ever feel obligated to share their pronouns. Do not be surprised or offended if other people do not. Many cisgender people are unfamiliar with the practice or do not see why they should do it, in which case the problem may be ignorance rather than bigotry. Trans and gender variant people may not always feel safe or comfortable sharing theirs. For example, a nonbinary person may fear awkwardness, judgment, or violence if they out themselves or use pronouns that are unfamiliar to someone, so they may choose not to share rather than misgender themselves. Some binary people, such as women applying for jobs in a male-dominated field, may want to avoid stereotypes and stigmas associated with a particular gender. Do not question or shame anyone who chooses not to share their pronouns. Instead, focus on your own behavior and educate anyone who asks.

To a large extent, it is up to individuals to avoid misgendering others; it is your responsibility to try to use people's pronouns correctly and to improve when you make mistakes. That said, there are a number of broad practices that libraries can adopt to minimize misgendering of employees and patrons. These policies are not a replacement for individual behavior during personal interactions, but they do make it easier for everyone concerned and cut down on misunderstandings. For the most part, all of the strategies below are elements of an overall environment that normalizes pronoun sharing. Success at this means that nobody will be singled out or outed when they try not to be misgendered.

Introductions

Verbal introductions are an important opportunity for pronoun sharing. Do this even if you share yours in your email or nametag or in other forms. Perhaps you are talking to people who have not seen or noticed. Even if you think everyone there knows your pronouns, sharing them acts as a reminder to others to do the same; it also lets people know that they can do so

EXAMPLE LANGUAGE

"Hello! I'm Stephen Krueger, the Access & Outreach Services Librarian. I use he/him or they/them pronouns."

"I'm Stephen. My pronouns are he/him or they/them. Welcome to the library!"

without being the only one. Whether you are meeting a new patron, presenting at a conference, or interviewing a job candidate, the model is essentially the same: state your pronouns after your name and move on.

This is becoming common practice in some places, but you may be the only person in a group to do it. Do not let this deter you; normalization takes time, and every time someone shares their pronouns it helps. It will almost certainly feel awkward at first, especially if you are the only one doing it. People may wonder or outright ask what you are doing, especially if you are cisgender or consistently pass as such. There may be some situations where you feel that the awkwardness is too much or that you do not want to start a conversation about gender. I am not going to tell you what to decide, but please remember that any awkwardness felt by cisgender people is probably minimal in comparison to the discomfort felt by a trans or gender variant person who is regularly misgendered and has to correct people. Knowing that people will not misgender you is a privilege, and you can use it to create a safer environment for people who lack it.

 Personal Experience

Every time I end up in a group doing introductions, I spend the time before my turn mentally preparing to share my pronouns. At this point, I know to expect one of several options.

1. I am the only person there to mention my pronouns. I feel anxiety from drawing attention to myself; sometimes, I worry that people think I am trying to shame them for forgetting, though I hope this is an irrational concern.

2. Some others in the group also share their pronouns, but it is only other trans and gender variant people. This is better in one way because we are not alone, but problematic because the pattern in which only trans people share pronouns is strengthened.

3. A few people, cisgender or a variety of gender identities, share their pronouns after I do, possibly because they were reminded that this is a thing. I feel more comfortable with every additional person.

4. Someone before me in the order shares their pronouns. I cannot express the relief I feel when this happens. Now I am no longer making a statement; on the contrary, I am normalizing the practice set by someone else.

5. The group leader mentions pronouns when they suggest information to share and states theirs to start. This is by far the best scenario, as it reminds everyone about the practice and people are much more likely to participate. Even if nobody else shares pronouns, I am not the odd one out for bringing it up.

6. Nobody, including me, shares pronouns. In the past, I might have simply forgotten (it does take practice to remember), but I am now in the habit. If I choose not to, it is because I feel unsafe or seriously uncomfortable doing so. Perhaps I am worried about a transphobic reaction. Perhaps there is a power dynamic present and I do not want to risk confusing or upsetting people. Perhaps I simply do not have the social energy to explain or worry about the reaction.

Regardless of how awkward it feels, I have no intention of stopping. While I am not at all closeted, most people assume that I am a cisgender man on first meeting. Correctly, they use *he/him* pronouns for me. I do not have to state my pronouns in order to avoid being misgendered, which is a privilege that many trans and gender variant people do not have. This was not always the case; I very clearly remember how much more stressful it was to share my pronouns knowing that I would be misgendered if I did not (and probably would be anyway). Then as now, I was almost invariably the only person in any given group to do so, but unlike now I could not choose not to unless I was prepared to be misgendered from the start. I share my pronouns now for normalization rather than self-preservation; I want to contribute to an environment where nobody is forced into the situation that I was.

 EXAMPLE LANGUAGE

"To start off, we'll go around and introduce ourselves. Let's do names, pronouns, and favorite soup. If you are uncomfortable sharing any of those things, please skip it. I'm Stephen. I use *he/him* or *they/them* pronouns, and my favorite soup is squash."

"Your pronouns are whatever personal pronouns you want people to use to refer to you. For example, you might say, 'Stephen is a librarian and he likes purple,' because I usually use *he/him* pronouns. Some people might not want you to guess their pronouns based on how you think they look, and clearly sharing them prevents misgendering so everyone can feel more comfortable. So my introduction sounds like this: I'm Stephen, and I use *he/him* or *they/them* pronouns."

If you are in a leadership position, whether for a large staff meeting or a small informal group, you can set an example and even encourage others to share their pronouns. Never require it; as previously mentioned, some people might not want to for a variety of perfectly legitimate reasons. Do, however, suggest it as part of the introduction and start by sharing yours if you are comfortable doing so. If you are incorporating some sort of ice-breaker, pronouns can be tucked into the rest of the information requested. This is an excellent way to normalize pronoun sharing; it also endorses the practice by having the leader of a group set an example. Do be prepared to explain if anyone asks or seems puzzled, as a lot of people are still unaware of why and how one would share pronouns.

 EXAMPLE LANGUAGE

"Remember how we included personal pronouns as part of the introduction today? I'd like you all to start doing that whenever you have a group meeting. You can also do it whenever you introduce yourself if you are comfortable with that. We're doing this to create a more inclusive work environment, especially for trans and gender variant people. If we all share our pronouns, then nobody has to out themselves by being the only one to do so. That said, nobody should feel obligated to share theirs if they are uncomfortable, so always make it optional. You can always email or talk to me privately about this if you want to. I really want to make sure that everyone feels comfortable here. We can also definitely talk about this now, especially if people have thoughts on how we can improve and create a more inclusive environment. Are there any questions or comments?"

"If you are running a meeting or event with introductions, please start including optional pronoun sharing. You don't have to share your own pronouns if you are uncomfortable, though you are certainly welcome to. Use language like this: 'Before we start, let's go around and introduce ourselves. You can let us know your position and what name and pronouns we should use for you. If you'd rather not share any of that information, just skip it.' We are trying to normalize pronoun sharing to make sure that people of all gender identities feel comfortable here. If you have any questions, please don't hesitate to ask; I want to make sure that we're doing this respectfully and that everyone has the information they need. Our LGBTQ+ Center and the website https://www.mypronouns.org/ are other good resources. If you have thoughts on how we can improve and create a more inclusive environment, please respond to this email."

Managers and other leaders can also encourage everyone in their department to adopt these techniques. For this, more explanation and resources should be provided so that people are equipped to answer questions in their own meetings. Always let them know where to go if they are confused or want more information.

Nametags and Such

Any written introduction can have pronouns after the name. This includes nametags (temporary or permanent), business cards, presentation slides, CVs, author or presenter bios, and probably many others. Anyone can share their pronouns in these forms; even if you are not concerned about people misgendering you, this normalizes pronoun sharing. It also lets trans and gender variant people know that you and/or your library are aware of the practice, which may help them feel more comfortable. Normalization of pronoun sharing is especially useful in these forms because they so often are used when interacting with strangers. It is much simpler to have people learn your pronouns by looking at your nametag than by having to correct them after they have misgendered you.

Personal Experience

At many work and social events, markers and stickers for guests to make their own nametags are supplied at the door. I always put my pronouns on these as well (usually unintelligibly, as my dreadful handwriting does not wed well with Sharpies). More than once now, other people have noticed this and gone back to add their own pronouns. I love it when this happens because they clearly understand why and how to share but simply did not think to do so—nothing was needed except the passing reminder that they got from seeing someone else do it.

As always, any form that asks for pronouns should be optional, open-ended, and equitable: everyone should be able to enter any pronouns they like without being required to do so. Keep this in mind if you are someone who controls what information goes onto something and how it looks. For example, if you are printing temporary nametags for an event, have an optional place for attendees to enter their pronouns and put those on if they do (see Chapter 7, "Conferences and Other Events," for more detailed information). If you are designing a business card, include a space for pronouns but do not make it an obvious gap if someone has chosen not to provide them. Remember that some neutral pronouns take up more text space than male or female ones and design accordingly.

Email Signatures

Email signatures are common, especially for work, and it is usually very easy to add your pronouns to them. There is no single correct format for this; anything that briefly and clearly states your pronouns is fine. My work email signature looks like this:

Stephen G. Krueger
Access & Outreach Services Librarian
Randolph College
Pronouns: he/him or they/them
skrueger@randolphcollege.edu
O: 434.947.8360
ORCID: 0000-0002-0607-2713

The Pronouns hyperlink goes to www.MyPronouns.org (Sakurai, 2017), a website that clearly explains what personal pronouns are and gives detailed examples about how to use them. Having a link there is not an original idea—I picked it up from a friend, and it is one of the suggestions on the website for sharing pronouns—but I like it very much. A lot of people are unaware of why one would put pronouns in an email signature, and this gives them a place to learn without having to ask.

Even if you can assume that people will correctly guess which pronouns you use, sharing them through your email signature is an unobtrusive way to let trans and gender variant people know that you are someone they do not have to explain themselves to. For anyone who cannot assume that (whether they are trans, nonbinary, or cisgender with an ambiguous name), sharing pronouns helps avoid confusion that might otherwise happen with long-distance communication. That said, there are perfectly valid reasons that someone might not want to do so. Perhaps someone wants to avoid disclosing their gender and knows that people may assume it based on their pronouns. Perhaps someone uses different pronouns with different people. As always with sharing pronouns, normalization is a great way to develop a more inclusive environment, but nobody of any gender identity should feel obligated to share their pronouns if they would prefer not to.

Some workplaces have a format for email signatures that they have all employees adopt. If you are in charge of such a thing, consider adding an optional pronoun field to the template (ideally with information attached to the template for those unfamiliar with the concept, such as the link above). This will demonstrate institutional values without forcing anyone to do anything that they are uncomfortable with, and it will provide a model for people who would not otherwise think about it. If you are an employee given such a template, suggest that the optional pronoun field be added. Even if it is not, add your own line. Be prepared to educate if a colleague, patron, or anyone else asks what it means.

ASKING FOR PRONOUNS

There are some situations in which you might ask for someone's pronouns. Perhaps it is a question on an application or other form; this can help limit misgendering. Perhaps you simply want to make sure that you are addressing people the way that they want. Any question about pronouns, verbal or written, should be all of the following things:

1. *Optional.* As discussed in the Sharing Pronouns section, there are many reasons why someone might not want to share their pronouns. Never force anyone to do so. If you are asking face-to-face, share your own pronouns first if you are comfortable doing so. If you are asking on a form, always make any question about gender or pronouns optional, and clearly note how the information will be used.

2. *Open-ended.* Always give people complete freedom in how they answer. Multiple-choice format invariably leaves something off and ends up othering people (sometimes by forcing them to literally select "Other").

3. *Equitable.* This seems like a good place to reiterate the running theme of this book: *You cannot tell someone's gender identity by looking at them.* If you ask one person about pronouns, do the same for everyone. Do not ask only people who you know or think are trans or gender variant. For one thing, you may not be correct, in which case you are perpetuating potentially offensive or harmful stereotypes of what trans people look like. Even if you are right, you single them out by asking. Depending on who else is present, you also risk outing them to other people (to reiterate another important concept, outing people is always rude and sometimes extremely dangerous for them).

❝▬▬ EXAMPLE LANGUAGE
▬▬❞

"My name is Stephen and my pronouns are he/him or they/them. Do you mind telling me what pronouns you want me to use for you?" *(Only ask this in a one-on-one conversation.)*

What pronouns should we use for you? (Optional. This information will be shared with the hiring committee so we do not misgender you.)

Pronouns (optional): _____

GETTING PRONOUNS WRONG

However good your intentions, you will probably end up misgendering someone at some point. This is not unusual; I have certainly done it and felt

> 66 — ■ **EXAMPLE LANGUAGE**
> —99
>
> "As he was saying—I'm sorry, as they were saying—"

terrible when I realized. Repeated misgendering is not acceptable, but do not stress about it if you slip occasionally. Instead, put your energy into improving (see Practicing Pronouns, above).

If You Catch Yourself or Are Corrected Immediately

1. Apologize, quickly and sincerely. Do not make a big deal out of it; that will draw more attention to the person, who may already feel uncomfortable.

2. Correct yourself. Repeat what you said using the right language.

3. Move on. After correcting yourself, continue as normal and try to avoid repeating the error. Do not try to defend yourself; making the situation about you is not helpful and will make everyone involved feel more uncomfortable, and everyone knows that mistakes happen. Dwelling on it centers your own experience at the expense of the other person's feelings, which is the opposite of allyship.

4. Improve. Misgendering once is not great, but it happens. Repetition indicates that you do not care enough about someone's gender identity to bother remembering or, worse, that you actively disrespect them. Do not expect anyone else to remind or educate you; it is your responsibility to practice and make yourself aware. See Figure 2.1.

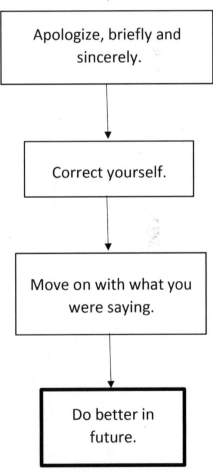

Apologize, briefly and sincerely.

↓

Correct yourself.

↓

Move on with what you were saying.

↓

Do better in future.

Figure 2.1. I accidentally misgendered someone. What should I do?

EXAMPLE LANGUAGE

"I realized that I misgendered you earlier and wanted to apologize. If you are comfortable doing so, please don't hesitate to correct me if it happens again."

If You Catch Yourself or Are Corrected Later

You can use the same techniques described above for a quick in-person or emailed apology, but keep it brief; your goal should be to let the person know that you respect them, not to earn their forgiveness or have an extended conversation about their gender identity. They are in no way obligated to respond, so do not bring it up again unless they do. Move on and improve in future.

When You Hear Someone Else Misgender a Person

1. Think about whether the misgendered person would want you to respond. You may not have all of the information, so speak up only if you know that is what they want. It may not be a mistake; there are a variety of reasons why someone might use different pronouns with different people. You may actually be the one misgendering them. They may not be out to everyone, in which case you would be outing them (which is horrifically rude at best and extremely dangerous at worst). They may be genderqueer, genderfluid, or otherwise prefer to use different language with different people. Some people use multiple sets of pronouns (for example, I use primarily *he/him* pronouns but have no objection to *they/them*).

2. If you know the misgendered person well enough, ask them about it privately. This may also be a way for you to learn if you have been misgendering them. They are not obligated to tell you, and you are certainly not entitled to any further information if they do not volunteer it. Do not ask how someone identifies (this is not the same thing as what pronouns they use). If you do not understand, do not express frustration or blame someone for your confusion;

 EXAMPLE LANGUAGE

"Please don't tell me anything you're not comfortable sharing, but I wanted to make sure I was using the name and pronouns that you wanted me to. Do you mind confirming what you would like me to use for you? Would you like me to say anything if I hear people using different ones?"

this can be extremely hurtful and makes the situation about your experience rather than theirs.

3. If you are certain that it was a mistake (that is, you know how a person wants to be referred to and heard someone use different language), still refrain from commenting until you know how the misgendered person wants you to respond. They may be uncomfortable with having someone corrected on their behalf even if they were misgendered.

4. Privately, ask what they would like you to do if you hear someone misgender them. As always, you are not entitled to a response at all, let alone any further information, so do not push if they hesitate to answer you.

 EXAMPLE LANGUAGE

"What would you like me to do if I hear someone misgendering you? Some options might be saying nothing, correcting them while you are present, or correcting them later when you aren't around. Would any of those be good, or would you prefer something else? It's fine if you prefer not to talk to me about this."

5. Do whatever they ask you to do. Do not decide that you know better—you do not. If they do not respond, continue to say nothing if you hear someone misgender them. Leave the door open for them to come to you if they decide something different; if this happens, change your behavior accordingly. Go by whatever they have most recently told you. See Figure 2.2.

 EXAMPLE LANGUAGE

"If things change or if you ever want to talk about any of this, please feel free to come to me."

UNKNOWN PRONOUNS

There will probably be situations when you do not know someone's pronouns. In those cases, avoid using gendered language entirely. In general, *they/them* pronouns can be applied to people of unknown gender identities as well as those who use them specifically as personal pronouns. When referring to someone you do not know, use a neutral descriptor such as "the patron." If you know the person's name of use, refer to them that way instead of assigning pronouns.

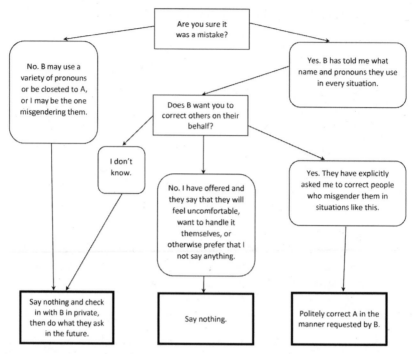

Figure 2.2. Person A misgendered Person B. What should I do?

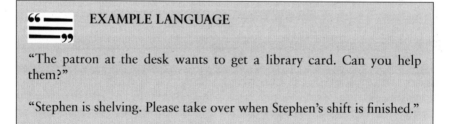

EXAMPLE LANGUAGE

"The patron at the desk wants to get a library card. Can you help them?"

"Stephen is shelving. Please take over when Stephen's shift is finished."

GENDER-NEUTRAL LANGUAGE

Pronouns are not the only way in which people can be misgendered. Say it with me: *You do not know someone's gender identity or pronouns unless they tell you.* Keep this in mind when referring to groups or individuals. Unless you are certain of the gender identity of everyone involved, use neutral language when talking to or about people. This applies to descriptions, honorifics, pronouns, and any other words that apply to individuals or groups. A lot of this language is so widely used that you may not even realize that it genders people, so try to take a step back and think about the terms that you use automatically. It may help to talk to your coworkers and start a collective initiative to eliminate gendered language; this way, you can share what you notice without anyone feeling accused or put on the spot.

Using gendered language to refer to groups ("boys," "girls," etc.) assumes that everyone in the group is of that gender identity. Instead, use neutral terms such as "first group" or "Group A." When addressing a mixed group, do not use binary terms such as "ladies and gentlemen." This excludes any nonbinary people who may be present. Try "everyone" or "folks" (as a native Vermonter who moved to the South, I have fully embraced "y'all" as a gender-neutral term). In group situations, gendered language is fine if you know that it is accurate, but this is only possible when you have learned the gender identity of every person present (as you should generally not ask people this, err on the side of neutral language).

When you describe or address an individual whom you do not know using a gendered term, you have assigned them a gender identity based on your own assumptions, potentially incorrectly. To avoid misgendering patrons and others, use neutral language when you do not explicitly know someone's gender identity. Pronouns are one form of this, as described above. Other gendered terms include descriptors ("the man over there") and honorifics such as "sir" or "miss." The honorifics can simply be eliminated, as dropping the word is less rude than misgendering someone. When describing an individual, use descriptors like "the person" or "the patron" instead of gendered terms.

Personal Experience

I do not know how many times I have been misgendered by strangers; it used to happen a lot, though it is rare now. My personal favorite is a hardware store employee who greeted me as "Sir . . . uh, ma'am . . . uh, whatever." To be fair, this was not an inaccurate description of my gender identity at the time, but the inadequacy of gendered language was abundantly clear.

Gender-neutral language may not feel natural at first. Most of us have years of habit to dismantle, and that takes time and practice. Do not worry if you make mistakes; as with pronouns, simply correct yourself, move on, and do better in future. If you are a manager, especially of people who work regularly with library patrons, provide your employees with training on how to use gender-neutral language in their work environment.

> 66 ══   **EXAMPLE LANGUAGE**
> ═══ 99

Instead of . . .	Say . . .
"Girls, follow me. Boys, wait here."	"Group One, follow me. Group Two, wait here."
"Welcome, ladies and gentlemen."	"Welcome, everyone."
"Excuse me, sir, you left your library card."	"Excuse me, you left your library card."
"The woman in the striped shirt"	"The person in the striped shirt"
"The new guy"	"The new employee"
"He is a new patron."	"They are a new patron."

QUICK FIXES

- Share your personal pronouns if you are comfortable doing so.
- Add optional pronoun fields to your institution's templates for email signatures, business cards, nametags, and so on.
- Incorporate pronoun sharing into meetings and other group activities.

LONG-TERM SOLUTIONS

- Practice using gender-neutral pronouns.
- Train staff to standardize pronoun sharing in all library activities.
- Develop a workplace culture in which you can point out when someone can use more inclusive language without their feeling attacked.

REFERENCES

Ford, Zack. "Laverne Cox: 'Loving Trans People Is a Revolutionary Act.'" *Think-Progress*, January 31, 2014, https://thinkprogress.org/laverne-cox-loving-trans -people-is-a-revolutionary-act-2b79c142ae69/.

Kehreim, Micah. "Improve Your Customer Service Skills: Go Gender Neutral!" American Library Association, accessed January 18, 2019, http://www.ala.org/ advocacy/diversity/odlos-blog/intersections-improve-your-customer-service-skills -go-gender-neutral.

Merriam-Webster. "Singular 'They.'" Merriam-Webster, accessed October 18, 2018, https://www.merriam-webster.com/words-at-play/singular-nonbinary-they.

Oxford University Press. "they, pron., adj., adv., and n." Oxford English Dictionary, accessed October 18, 2018, http://www.oed.com/view/Entry/200700.

Sakurai, Shige. "MyPronouns.org: Resources on Personal Pronouns." MyPronouns .org, accessed October 15, 2018, https://www.mypronouns.org/.

Shlasko, Davey. *Trans Allyship Workbook*. Think Again Training, 2017.

3

Personal Information

WHY IS PERSONAL INFORMATION COMPLICATED?

Name Changes

In the United States, most people have a legal name and a name of use. For some, these are identical. For others, they are not. There are any number of reasons that a person might not go by their legal name. For trans and gender variant people, a very common reason is that the legal name assigned at birth is associated with a gender identity that is not our own.

Community Voices

It turns out that there is a lot in, and to, a name. For a wide variety of reasons, I've never legally changed my name. It's always just seemed easier to keep the name my parents assigned to me when I was born and go from there. Besides, my first name is spelled exactly like that great lady of the screen, Katharine Hepburn. How cool is that? Still, other than blood family, everyone calls me JJ. It's on my employer-provided business cards, in my email signature, and on every publication I publish. And yet, my employer has no way to change my name in the system so that my preferred name shows up on directories and so forth. To say that it is aggravating is a gross understatement. As my legal name is feminine, it means that when people are looking for me, they expect to see a woman, not a man and so there is always a brief moment of awkwardness. Put my legal name on my paychecks. In this day and age, I should be able to be called what I want.
—JJ Pionke, University of Illinois at Urbana-Champaign

The requirements for changing one's legal name vary from one state to another. It is often a lengthy and costly process, so not everyone is able to do it even if they want to. The 2015 U.S. Transgender Survey reported that 64 percent of its respondents had not tried to change their legal name (James et al., 2016, p. 83). Of these, 35 percent said that they could not afford it; others were not ready (40 percent), did not have a name conflicting with their gender identity (28 percent), feared outing themselves (24 percent), or did not know how (24 percent). Note the relatively small number of people who were comfortable with their original legal name, compared to the majority who either had changed it or wanted to but could not. Libraries may not be able to help change those numbers (though we could look into providing information on the name change process in our location). However, we can take steps to help those who do not use their legal name feel more comfortable in libraries, whether they are patrons or employees or both.

Personal Experience

I was assigned female at birth and given a name that is generally used for women. Eventually, I became uncomfortable with it because I did not identify as female. I went by a gender neutral name for a while before choosing my current one and getting a legal name change. All in all, there was a period of approximately four years when my name of use differed from my legal name, plus many more years before that when I was vaguely uncomfortable with my name but was not sure why. During this time, I felt increasing levels of discomfort when people called me by my legal name. By the end, when I had adopted *he/him* pronouns, calling me by my legal name both outed me to anyone present and indicated that the speaker did not respect my gender identity (as well as implicitly encouraging others to do the same).

I hesitated to change my legal name, partly because of the complicated process required and partly because I did not want to participate in the system of charging trans people additional costs for existing. However, I was also starting my second year of library school, and I decided that job hunting would be difficult enough without having my name out me at every step. I cannot speak for other locations, but in Orange County, North Carolina, in 2017, a legal name change cost around $200 plus several days of missed work to go to the courthouse and Social Security office. The process took perhaps six months; it included fingerprinting, state and federal background checks, a public posting of my current and intended legal names, and notarized affidavits from friends confirming that I was who I said I was. After receiving the court order of the change (and then a replacement because they had written my new name incorrectly), it took several visits to the Social Security office and DMV to get new identification. The new driver's license was not comparatively expensive, but my new passport cost an additional $170. Two years later and counting, I still have trouble with everything from Spotify to banking, as many companies and institutions have a difficult or nonexistent process for changing account names.

What really struck me was how many barriers existed to getting a name change. I had my own transportation, a job that let me take days off, and the financial ability to miss work and pay the direct costs (even if it was through student loans). The process was deeply inconvenient even with those resources; it would be far more difficult or impossible without them. The instructions were not available online, so the first step was to take time off work to drive to the courthouse and pay $3 for a print copy of them (this was the smallest cost, but having to pay for information about a government process filled my librarian heart with rage). There was also an enormous amount of stress involved, as every step required outing myself to a stranger.

Legal Gender

Legal gender is even more complicated. It is assigned at birth and appears on driver's licenses, passports, birth certificates, and other documentation. As of 2019, all but five U.S. states provide only male and female options, which means that people who are not one of those two genders cannot accurately identify themselves. As with names, the process for changing one's legal gender varies by state, and it does not happen all at once. Changing the gender marker on a driver's license is a completely different thing from changing a birth certificate or any other documentation. I am not going to describe all of the possible variations; if you are curious about the requirements in your state, look it up in the ID Documents Center (National Center for Transgender Equality, n.d.). In most states, the gender marker on a birth certificate can be changed with a court order and/or a doctor's letter; some places require proof of surgery, others do not. Tennessee is the only state to explicitly prohibit changing the gender on a birth certificate for trans people (TN Code § 68-3-203(d)). It is possible to change the gender marker on a driver's license anywhere in the United States, though the requirements for that vary as well. The National Center for Transgender Equality (n.d.) has graded each state on how cumbersome those requirements are. Three states and Washington, D.C. earn an A+ for requiring no doctor's note and having a gender-neutral option. Ten states earn an F for requiring proof of surgery, a court order, or an amended birth certificate.

Personal Experience

Changing the gender on my driver's license required a signed letter from a doctor confirming that I did, in fact, identify as male. Fortunately, my state (Virginia, at the moment) does not require proof of surgery, but it was still inconvenient and humiliating and would not have been possible if I had not had access to a supportive doctor. I am honestly not sure what my official legal gender is at the moment because I have not changed it on any other documentation. I will likely change my passport at some point, and I was born in a state that permits me to change my birth certificate if I choose to, but both processes require more money, time, and emotional energy than I am willing to commit to them at this point.

TYPES OF PERSONAL INFORMATION

Name

When you ask for a person's name on an application or other form, think carefully about what information you need. Do you want to know what to call someone or how to enter them in your system? Name of use should be sufficient. Ask for someone's legal name only if you absolutely need to know it. For many trans and gender variant people, sharing a legal name effectively outs us; even if we do not mind being out as trans or gender variant, talking about our legal name can be a very uncomfortable experience. Therefore, you should not ask for someone's legal name unless you have a specific reason. Never ask the legal name without also asking the name of use.

When creating or updating a form, be clear about what you are asking. If you need only name of use, specify as much by writing "Name of Use" instead of "Name." This term might be unfamiliar to some people, so include a definition. If you absolutely need to know the legal name as well, put that field second so that name of use takes priority when people review the form. Include a note explaining how that legal name will be used and who will see it. Only those who really need to should see the legal name; everyone else should see only the name of use. If necessary, ask for previous legal names; this gives trans and gender variant people (as well as anyone else who has changed their name) a way to be sure that they will not be rejected because of a name change. As with the current legal name, explain why you need this information and who will see it. With every step, think about how your form will feel to a person who will out themselves if they have to share a current or past legal name. Sometimes you do need this information, but you can be thoughtful about how you collect it. Make sure that your actual

Community Voices

It all starts with a name. It can be difficult to get used to referring to someone by a new name. We have experienced this when someone gets married and changes their name. It takes a while. Unfortunately, too often it's not as easy when a transgender or non-binary person has changed their name. On one hand, some people commit the "mistake" with malice and intent. On the other, the insulted party reacts in haste and anger. Civility on both sides can bring about the harmony that is helpful both in workplaces and in social situations. Tirades generally only serve to arm those anti-trans people with real-life circumstances that demonstrate our weakest links. Insults bring about harm and resentment toward cis people. There are two sides to the equation. Get the name right, please. And when it's not, we need to be patient and take the high road.

—Paige Flanagan

practices match what you tell people on the form; it is unacceptable to inform someone that their legal name will be kept confidential if this is not actually true.

Pronouns

In some cases, it is appropriate to ask for someone's pronouns on a form or survey. This should always be an optional question, as people of any gender identity may have legitimate reasons for preferring not to share their pronouns. Include a pronouns field if it will be useful to the person or to those interacting with them. One example is job applications so that search committees can make sure to avoid misgendering candidates. Another is event registration so that pronouns can be printed on name badges. As with names, explain who sees the information and how it will be used; this will help people decide what to say. On a form like a library card application, there is probably no purpose in asking for pronouns (unless they are included in the patron's account somewhere, which is rare).

Gender

If you are considering asking about gender on an application or survey, think very carefully about whether you actually need that information. Unlike name and pronouns, this is not something you need to know to refer to a person respectfully. Even if you phrase the question inclusively, it is not something you should ask unless you have a concrete reason for doing so. Such reasons do exist, so if you do have one, say so. Explain why you are asking about gender and who will see the responses. Then be very thought-ful in how you write the question. What information are you trying to collect? If you are surveying a group to assess its demographics, perhaps you want to ask only for gender identity. If you want to ask if people are trans or gender variant, make it a separate question.

The only way to ask about gender in a truly inclusive way is to make every question open ended. Even legal gender should be open ended, as some countries and states have implemented a variety of nonbinary options so some people may have a legal gender that is not male or female. That said, there are some situations in which open-ended questions are not possible. Perhaps you are supplying data about your applicants to an organization that will only accept binary genders. In that case, keep the gender identity field open ended and use multiple-choice for the legal gender. I object to multiple-choice gender identity questions strongly enough that I will not provide any examples. They invariably leave someone out, sometimes literally othering them by making "other" the best option. Forcing someone to choose between seven options is not better than forcing them to choose between two if none of them fit. Providing more options is great for people who see themselves represented, but those who are not listed can feel even more erased.

Honorific

You may want to ask for an honorific, especially in a formal context such as a job application. This question should always be optional. Since so many different ones exist (academic titles, military ranks, etc.), open ended is the best format so you don't leave anyone out. If you must use multiple-choice, make sure to include *Mx.* (usually pronounced like "mix"), which is the gender-neutral equivalent of *Mr./Ms.* This ensures that people are not forced to opt out or incorrectly label themselves. *Mx.* can also be used by people who identify as male or female but do not want to share their gender.

UNIQUE IDENTIFIERS

In addition to inclusive practices for asking the names of new patrons and employees, develop a system for changes to someone's name of use and/or legal name. Unique identifiers are one way to do this. They should be gender neutral and not based on the individual's name. This may already exist in your system in the form of library card numbers (for patrons) and ID numbers (for employees). If so, make sure that other information can be easily changed. If possible, people should be able to change it themselves by accessing their account online; this saves them from having to share information on their transition in person if they are not comfortable doing so. Talk to your Human Resources and IT departments about this option. Sample language is provided below if people do need to request a name change.

As pointed out by Virginia Commonwealth University's Gender-Inclusive Library Workgroup Report (White et al., 2018), an excellent example of an inclusive system is ORCID (Open Researcher and Contributor ID), a non-profit organization that creates unique identifiers for scholars. Accounts are free, and each member gets a page showing all of their published work. The primary name can be edited by the individual, so it is easy to update while still showing work published under a different name. In addition, there is an optional "Also known as" field, so one can list previous names if desired. One potential issue for trans and gender variant scholars, as well as any others who have changed their name of use or legal name, is the ability of readers to find material published under a different name. ORCID's unique identifier system, combined with the ease of self-identifying current and past names, is a simple and elegant solution.

HOW TO COLLECT PERSONAL INFORMATION

Patron Application

Ask for name of use, and include an explanatory note so that patrons and library employees are not confused. Do not ask for gender or pronouns. Do not ask for legal name unless your system has a practical reason for requiring it; if this is the case, consider in future whether another method will work instead. If all you want is to confirm identity before accepting a new patron, you can check ID or proof of residency and then put the name of use on the account; the fact that the account exists acts as confirmation of identity, so it does not need the legal name attached to it.

❝▬▬ EXAMPLE LANGUAGE
▬▬❞

Name of use* _____

Name of use is what you want to be called for in-person and written communications. It does not need to match your legal name.

Job Posting

Ask for name of use and legal name, with a note that the search committee will see the name of use and the legal name will be seen only by those

" ≡≡   EXAMPLE LANGUAGE

Honorific (optional): _____

Name of use*: _____

Current legal name: _____

Past legal name(s) (optional): _____

Name of use is what you want to be called in person and on written communications; this is what the search committee will see. Legal name(s) are used for background checks; Human Resources personnel will see this information, but it will not be shared with anyone else.

Name of use*: _____

Name of use is what you want to be called in person and on written communications. If we need your legal name for a background check or other reason, we will ask for it later.

Pronouns (optional)*: _____

*Your pronouns will be shared with the search committee and others involved with the interview process.

Gender*:

   Gender identity (optional): _____

   Legal gender (optional): M ___ F ___ Other ___

*Gender information will be anonymized and reported to the Equal Opportunity Employment Commission. It will not be shared with anyone involved in the interview process.

"Application Instructions: On your application materials, please put whatever name you would like us to call you by. If we need your legal name for a background check, we will let you know. Feel free to let us know your pronouns as well so we can be sure to refer to you correctly."

who need it. Alternately, ask for the name of use and mention that HR may ask for the legal name later for background checks and such. Honorifics and pronouns should be marked as optional so that people are not forced to identify their gender. If a gender section is included, clearly explain who sees the responses. If you ask for materials such as a CV and cover letter, tell applicants that they should put their name of use on them and that you will ask for the legal name as needed. This is also a good place to suggest pronoun sharing, which will indicate that applicants can do so without damaging their chances of getting the job.

Surveys

Ask for only the information that you need. For example, do not ask about gender unless you plan to do something with that information. Be specific and inclusive with your questions so that anyone who wants to can respond accurately, and make gender questions optional so that people can still participate if they do not want to share their gender.

---

66 ═══   EXAMPLE LANGUAGE
═══99

Gender identity (optional): _____

Legal gender (optional): _____

Do you consider yourself to be trans or gender variant, including but not limited to transgender, nonbinary, agender, genderfluid, genderqueer, and other non-cisgender identities? (optional) _____

Name Change Form

Employees and patrons may want to report a change to their name of use and/or legal name. Provide a clear way to do this. Ask only for the information you need to find and update the account.

> **" ═══ EXAMPLE LANGUAGE**
> **═══"**
>
> Employee name change form*:
>
> Employee ID number _____
>
> Has your name of use changed? No ___ Yes, to _____
>
> Has your legal name changed? No___ Yes, to _____
>
> *Name of use is what will show on your account and all communications; legal name will be used where necessary (paychecks, health insurance, etc.) and seen only by Human Resources personnel. Please contact [HR contact information] if you have questions about reporting name changes.
>
> Patron name change form:
>
> Library card number: _____
>
> New name of use*: _____
>
> *Name of use is what you want to be called for in-person and written communications. It does not need to match your legal name.

EMPLOYEE TRAINING

All employees who work with personal information should be trained in gender-inclusive practices. This means general awareness of why these practices are important; it also means education on the specifics of your systems so that they can accurately and respectfully answer questions and process information. The best name change system in the world is useless if circulation assistants do not know to tell patrons that it exists. Write clear instructions for all of the situations in which a library employee interacts with the personal information of a patron or other employee and make these instructions part of training. It also helps to create and run practice scenarios, especially with circulation assistants and others who will be doing this work face-to-face.

QUICK FIXES

- Revise name fields on patron and job applications and include explanatory notes.
- Add note to job postings telling applicants to put their name of use.
- Add optional pronoun field when relevant.
- Revise gender questions and add explanatory note.

LONG-TERM SOLUTIONS

- Assess existing forms to determine what information is actually needed.
- Develop and publicize a clear system for name changes.
- Train employees about inclusive practices for collecting personal information.

REFERENCES

James, Sandy E., Jody L. Herman, Susan Rankin, Mara Keisling, Lisa Mottet, and Ma'ayan Anafi. *The Report of the 2015 U.S. Transgender Survey*. Washington, DC: National Center for Transgender Equality, 2016.

National Center for Transgender Equality. "ID Documents Center." National Center for Transgender Equality, last modified February 2019, https://transequality.org/documents/.

"ORCID." Accessed January 19, 2019. www.orcid.org.

White, Erin, Donna E. Coghill, M. Theresa Doherty, Liam Palmer, and Steve Barkley. *Gender-Inclusive Library Workgroup Report*. Richmond, VA: Virginia Commonwealth University, 2018. https://scholarscompass.vcu.edu/libraries_task/1/.

4

Restrooms

For many trans people, public restroom use is a source of stress and anxiety. I believe that the following findings from the 2015 U.S. Transgender Survey (James et al., 2016) speak for themselves:

- Nearly one-quarter (24 percent) of respondents said that someone had questioned or challenged their presence in a restroom in the past year.
- Nearly one in ten (9 percent) respondents reported that someone denied them access to a restroom in the past year.
- One in eight (12 percent) respondents were verbally harassed, physically attacked, or sexually assaulted when accessing or using a restroom in the past year.
- More than half (59 percent) avoided using a public restroom in the past year because they were afraid of having problems.
- Nearly one-third (32 percent) limited the amount they ate or drank to avoid using the restroom in the past year.
- Eight percent (8 percent) reported having a urinary tract infection, kidney infection, or another kidney-related problem in the past year as a result of avoiding restrooms. (James et al., 2016, p. 225)

Restroom use is such a pervasive everyday event that few cis people think twice about it. When every instance comes with the risk of judgment, verbal confrontation, or outright physical attack, the stress and fear affects every situation in which one might have to use a restroom. This is the case in unfamiliar places, but it can also be true in everyday situations such as at work, school, or the local library.

Personal Experience

The first time someone seriously questioned my presence in a restroom, I was eighteen. It was at a folk music festival in a town that prided itself on its progressive nature. I spent the next decade being helpfully informed by all sorts of people that I was in the wrong place. "This is the *ladies'* room" was the most common form, usually coming from cis women. A helpful man at a bar called, "Hey, dude, that's the girls'" as he saw me go in. Once, terrifyingly, an armed security guard followed me into the restroom at my public library. Having seen me from a distance, he thought it appropriate to enter and announce that it was the women's room. When I responded, from inside a stall, that I knew this and was in the correct place, he left reluctantly. I stopped going to the library when that guard was working.

The common thread in all of these instances is that I was using the women's room, which matched the sex assigned to me at birth. I had not yet come out as transgender, even to myself. Entering the men's room had never occurred to me, and there was rarely a neutral option. I was in the space that I had always been told to use and had no reason not to, and yet people repeatedly told me that I should not be there.

I was living in North Carolina when HB2 passed, making it literally illegal for me to use the men's room. Two instances from that period stick in my mind. One was the comment of someone that I assumed to be the mother of a student, as nobody on campus had openly questioned my restroom use since I had started at UNC. She stared at me as I entered; after I had gone into a stall, she paused her phone conversation to call, "Am I in the right bathroom?" (She clearly knew full well that she was.) It shook me more than I expected; we were in the main library, a place where I worked and studied every day, but a stranger's entitlement had made it a space where I was unwelcome. HB2 was in effect, which meant that I was legally required to use that restroom.

The second memory I have from that period goes the other way. I found myself washing my hands beside another person. My usual habit of getting in and out as quickly as possible and avoiding all eye contact was interrupted when I found that the person next to me presented as androgynously as I did. I do not know their gender identity—I only sort of knew mine at that point—but I clearly remember the relief of realizing that they were not going to question my presence. I saw them come to the same conclusion. We did not speak, but we sort of grinned sidelong at each other, a small affirmation that we were both safe. This really should not have been a memorable moment. However, using gendered restrooms was so stressful that doing so without fear of confrontation was notable in itself.

Almost every trans or gender variant person I know has too many of these stories to count. Nearly all of them could have been prevented by inclusive restroom design and staff training. Libraries already stand apart as one of the few places where people can use restrooms for free; they should also take steps to ensure that everyone can do so comfortably and safely. The following guidelines describe how libraries and library workers can minimize the negative experiences that trans and gender variant people so often associate with public restrooms.

IF YOUR LIBRARY HAS ALL-GENDER RESTROOMS

Gendered restrooms are those designated for use by only men or women. *All-gender restrooms* (also known as *gender-neutral* or *unisex*) are single-occupancy or multistall restrooms that may be used by anyone, regardless of legal gender or gender identity. If you already have all-gender restrooms in your library, that is excellent! The most difficult part is already done. Just having them in the building, however, is not enough; people must know that they are there and be able to find them easily. Signage should clearly indicate what types of restrooms are available and how to get to them. This is not exclusively a gender issue; accessibility should also be noted so that everyone can easily find a restroom that they can use. Floor directories, maps, and other information should note restroom types and locations.

Having a single all-gender restroom does not mean a library should not add more. Even if you already have one or more available, consider building others or converting existing gendered ones. Especially do this if the current all-gender options are out of the way (either literally difficult to get to or in a designated space such as the children's area), not wheelchair accessible, or otherwise limiting. Any single-occupancy restrooms should be all-gender, and multistall ones can also be converted. Renovations or other building projects often bring the opportunity to add or increase inclusive options.

Be aware that people sometimes decide to use single-occupancy restrooms for changing, phone calls, smoking, or other non-restroom-related activities. This is an issue when there is only one restroom that some people can use—that is, if it is the only accessible or all-gender restroom. To limit long waiting periods for people who specifically need an accessible and/or all-gender space, develop clear policies about what behavior is acceptable. As with signage, focus on what the space is used for, not who uses it. A better long-term solution is to add more all-gender and accessible restrooms so that people who need them are never limited to only one option.

The presence of all-gender restrooms does not mean that trans and gender variant people are obliged to use them. Conversely, it may seem tempting to discourage cisgender people from using all-gender restrooms, but this is not an effective approach. It suggests that neutral spaces are only for trans people, which is not the case; this can also further imply that trans and gender variant people should not be using gendered spaces, which is deeply problematic. Designating trans-only spaces automatically outs anyone who uses them. Ideally, everyone should be able to use whichever restroom they are most comfortable in without having their presence there questioned; this goes for cis people using all-gender restrooms as well as for trans and gender variant people using gendered ones. Remember that nobody can tell anyone else's gender identity without asking them. Never tell anyone, however you think they identify, which restroom they should use. Focus on behavior and services rather than policing gender.

IF YOUR LIBRARY DOES NOT HAVE ALL-GENDER RESTROOMS

Providing all-gender restrooms should be the main goal, even if it takes some time to achieve. Other measures may go some way to create an inclusive environment, but forcing people to choose a gendered restroom is not an equitable situation. There will always be some who feel uncomfortable or unsafe with the binary options. Converting existing single-occupancy restrooms is usually fairly easy and uncontroversial, so start there if any are available. See the "Signage" section below for information on how to label the space. Make sure to update all directional signage as well as any building maps or directories. Educate employees, including security and cleaning staff, about the change, and make sure everyone has the chance to ask questions if they are unsure about the purpose of an all-gender restroom. Converting multistall restrooms can be more complicated, but it is definitely feasible and should be considered. The *Library Journal* article "Inclusive Restroom Design" (Schwartz, 2018) contains some successful examples, as well as excellent guidelines for converting and creating all-gender restrooms in libraries.

Until all-gender restrooms can be added, there are ways to make gendered restrooms more inclusive. Develop policies and post them by all restrooms (see the following section for details). Put wastebaskets in the stalls of men's as well as women's rooms. Train all library workers and security personnel in how to give directions without assuming gender identity and in what to do if someone complains (see "Giving Directions" and "Addressing Concerns," below). These practices can all be continued even after all-gender restrooms are added, as their presence does not preclude making gendered spaces inclusive.

POLICIES

The Occupational Safety and Health Administration (n.d.) and the Human Rights Campaign Foundation (2016) both recommend that companies adopt policies stating that all employees and customers may use the

EXAMPLE LANGUAGE

Restroom policy: "All patrons and employees of the library are encouraged to use the restroom that best corresponds to their gender identity (for example, the men's or the all-gender restroom for a person identifying as male). The decision of which to use should be left up to the individual."

Sign (to be placed outside each restroom): "All patrons and employees of the library are encouraged to use the restroom that best corresponds to their gender identity. Men's and women's restrooms are located on the third floor, and accessible all-gender restrooms are located on the first and fourth floors."

restroom that best corresponds with their gender identity; both say explicitly that restroom choice should be left up to the individual. Libraries are no exception to this. Whether your library has all-gender restrooms or not, make sure that there is an official inclusive restroom policy. Make this publicly available on the website and anywhere else policies are documented, but also post a printed version by the restrooms themselves. This is also a good place to list the locations of different restroom options so that everyone can determine where they feel most comfortable. Having a policy is insufficient if it is not backed by employee behavior, so all library workers should be educated about what the policy means and why it is important. If your library has security guards, volunteers, or external cleaning staff, make sure that they receive the same information. Particularly emphasize that they are not to tell anyone to leave a restroom based on their appearance.

SIGNAGE

Whether you are building new all-gender restrooms, converting gendered ones, or updating existing signs, think carefully about how you label them. A common "neutral" restroom sign shows both the traditional male and female figures, which I cannot help but think of as "person" and "skirt-person." This does not acknowledge nonbinary genders; it also perpetuates stereotypes for everyone, including cis people. A presumably well-intended alternative adds a third figure composed of a combination of the other two, but I personally rather detest the way this represents gender.

Some signs, presumably in an attempt to be funny or cute, show a variety of human, alien, and fantastical creatures, often with text like "Whatever, just wash your hands." In general, equating noncisgender people with

This "neutral" restroom sign perpetuates the gender binary and erases nonbinary identities.

An ideal restroom sign depicting relevant information about the space.

inhuman creatures is not ideal, but my real problem with this approach is how confusing it can be, especially to non-English speakers. Usability is always important, and overcomplicating signage for all-gender restrooms draws attention to them instead of normalizing them. Make sure that the signage reflects all languages used by your patrons so that everyone understands the restroom options and policies.

As with most situations concerning gender, I think that the best approach is to avoid the question of gender identity entirely. Instead, focus on what the space is used for. The best solution by far is to simply show the toilet symbol; this shows the purpose of the room rather than who should use it. Urinals, changing stations, accessibility, and any other elements can be similarly indicated.

WASTEBASKETS

This is one of those issues that simply does not occur to people if they have not experienced it, so I am going to be blunt: People of all gender identities may menstruate. In my experience, most men's restrooms do not have wastebaskets in the stalls, which makes it difficult to throw away pads and tampons without bringing them into the public area (and thus potentially outing oneself, which can be uncomfortable or dangerous). One very easy way to make restrooms more trans-friendly is to put wastebaskets in the stalls of all restrooms, gendered or not. Please do this. It is not difficult.

GIVING DIRECTIONS

One common microaggression occurs when someone assumes that they know which restroom another person should use. By directing someone to a specific restroom, you have assigned them a gender identity, potentially incorrectly (unless you already know how they identify). As discussed elsewhere in this book, misgendering someone is very rude. An interaction like this may make a patron unwilling to talk to you again; they may also feel uncomfortable using any restroom around you, as you have indicated which one you think is appropriate. Fortunately, it is extremely easy to avoid this: when someone asks for directions, tell them all of the options available so that they can choose for themselves. This habit also benefits people who may be asking for another person and not just themselves. If you are in a leadership position, make sure that all staff are trained to give directions this way. Even if not, you can set an example for coworkers by doing it yourself and explaining why if they ask.

 EXAMPLE LANGUAGE

Instead of "The women's room is over there," say "The men's room is there, the women's room is there, and the all-gender restroom is there." Do this for everyone, even if the directions are complicated; it will come naturally with practice.

ADDRESSING CONCERNS

In an ideal world, everyone would use the restroom that they feel most comfortable in, and nobody would question anyone else's decision on the matter. Unfortunately, this is not always the case. A lot of people do make assumptions about gender, and some feel entitled to act upon those assumptions. Library employees should be prepared to respond to patrons and coworkers who complain about sharing space with trans and gender variant people, or who tell others that they are in the wrong place. The Human Rights Campaign Foundation (2016) offers guidelines on what to say in this situation. These are designed for managers, but any employee can adapt them as needed. First, listen and acknowledge the concern. Even if you do

EXAMPLE LANGUAGE

"Our policy is that everyone can use the restroom that matches their gender identity. Are they behaving inappropriately? If not, there is no reason to ask them to leave. You are welcome to use a different restroom if you prefer."

not agree, sharing that will probably not help anything. Then refocus the issue by shifting the conversation to behavior rather than identity. Remind the complainer that, as long as no inappropriate behavior is taking place (and simply existing in a space does not count), everyone has the right to equitable restroom access. Refer to the policy to reinforce the values of inclusion and access for all. If they remain unhappy, remind them that they can choose to alter their own behavior by waiting or using a different restroom themselves.

When dealing with complaints like this, never suggest that someone who is behaving appropriately should be forced to leave a restroom so that someone else can feel more comfortable. Library staff probably cannot change the mind of a transphobic patron or coworker, but they can make sure that people who are using the space appropriately are not harassed for simply existing. Posting signage (see "Policies," above) can help establish that environment and minimize harassment and complaints.

NOT JUST A TRANS ISSUE

Inclusive restrooms do not affect only trans and gender variant people. There are plenty of instances (parents with small children or people with disabilities, for example) where someone needs assistance; gendered restrooms can be very limiting in these cases, as the person helping may not be of the same gender identity as the primary restroom user. Gendered restrooms are also simply inefficient, as one may have an extended line and another none at all. Signage often perpetuates outdated stereotypes, most often equating women with skirts. Cisgender people who do not present in those stereotypical binary ways are sometimes misgendered and asked to leave the restroom that matches their gender identity. The lack of changing tables in some men's restrooms perpetuates stereotypes in a much more concrete way by assuming that only women take care of children and making it more difficult for men to do so. Removing gender from restrooms resolves all sorts of issues that are not exclusive to trans and gender variant people.

QUICK FIXES

- Convert any gendered single-occupancy restrooms to all-gender ones (usually, all this requires is a sign change, some staff education, and revision of building maps or directories).
- Put wastebaskets in the stalls of all restrooms.
- Train staff to tell people about all available restrooms when asked for directions instead of assuming the asker's gender identity.
- Post clear signage so all restroom options can be easily found.

LONG-TERM SOLUTIONS

- Use signage that does not perpetuate the gender binary.
- Develop an inclusive restroom policy and post signage by restrooms (especially gendered ones) explaining that everyone can use whichever best fits their gender identity.
- Educate library workers and others (security, housekeeping, volunteers) about the policy and how to apply it.
- Add more all-gender restrooms to your library (convert multistall gendered ones and build new ones).

REFERENCES

Human Rights Campaign Foundation. "Sample Restroom Policy." Human Rights Campaign, last modified 2016, https://assets2.hrc.org/files/assets/resources/HRC_Sample_Restroom_Policy_and_Talking_Points_for_Managers.pdf?_ga=2.218362385.903395567.1544499798-986011610.1544499798.

James, Sandy E., Jody L. Herman, Susan Rankin, Mara Keisling, Lisa Mottet, and Ma'ayan Anafi. *The Report of the 2015 U.S. Transgender Survey*. Washington, DC: National Center for Transgender Equality, 2016.

Occupational Safety and Health Administration. "Best Practices: A Guide to Restroom Access for Transgender Workers." Occupational Safety and Health Administration (accessed December 10, 2018), https://www.dol.gov/asp/policy-development/TransgenderBathroomAccessBestPractices.pdf.

Schwartz, Meredith. "Inclusive Restroom Design." *Library Journal* (May 8, 2018).

5

Job Postings and Interviews

A note on scope: Any discussion of legal requirements and government policies refers to the United States as of early 2019. Other countries may have different legislation, and the legislation described here may change over time.

The hiring process is an important component of an inclusive work environment. From the job posting itself, to pronoun sharing in the phone interview, to the restrooms available to visiting applicants, there are a variety of ways in which potential employers can welcome trans and gender variant candidates to their libraries.

ADVERTISING AND JOB DESCRIPTIONS

Job hunting is stressful for most people, but there are ways in which it can be especially difficult for trans and gender variant folks. Fortunately, most of these difficulties can be easily countered by employers. In general, make yourself aware of the concerns that trans and gender variant people feel when entering a potential workplace and design the hiring process to eliminate those concerns.

For LGBTQ+ people, coming out is not a one-time event. Every new situation and every single person you meet comes with a set of questions. These questions vary from person to person, but mine usually look something like this: Is it safe to be out? If so, does it matter to me whether they know my gender identity or orientation? If so, what is the best way to share that information? By safety, I do not mean only the lack of physical danger. Fear of violence is an awful but relatively uncomplicated reason to stay closeted. Much more complex is the worry that coming out to a supervisor will limit promotion opportunities, or that coming out during a job interview will cost you the offer. With this in mind, employers can indicate from the beginning

Community Voices

*Whenever I speak or write about my experiences iden-
tifying as non-binary trans as it relates to libraries and
employment, it feels important to mention that privilege
makes it much easier for me to feel comfortable sharing
my identity during an interview. I am white, I have never been unemployed, I have years of experience working in libraries, and I've been
fortunate to work in spaces that have non-discrimination agreements
(ENDA [Employment Non-Discrimination Act]).*

*Like so many people who identify as queer and trans, I came out in
stages. I began my career in libraries nearly two decades ago, and in
time I essentially transitioned, albeit very slowly, on the job. I've navi-
gated coming out as queer, a legal name change, and top surgery, and
I've dealt with the repercussions—the questions, the commentary, and
the isolation—that followed each of those changes. But none of those
experiences prepared me for the challenges trans folks face when they
apply for jobs.*

*Job interviews are incredibly fraught environments that can desta-
bilize even the most seasoned and prepared interviewees. Though I'm
usually comfortable speaking about my identity, I have experienced a
number of situations that were troubling; I've arrived at an in-person
interview and could instantly sense that I wasn't what the search committee expected—my name is one that is traditionally male, but as a
non-binary person, I don't typically pass as male; I've made it to the
final round of interviews for positions, and they've asked for transcripts,
one of which still lists my birth name, a name that I've not used in
nearly a decade, and the interviewers used my birth name repeatedly.
Those interview situations were extremely difficult, but even more frus-
trating, they were avoidable; if as a profession, we are truly committed
to advancing equity and inclusion, it's important to understand that
those initiatives require more than a mention in our mission statements,
they require action.*

—Max G. Bowman, they/them, librarian

that trans and gender variant people are welcome. There are a few ways
to do this before they even talk to the search committee. I look for three
things when I apply for jobs: an Equal Opportunity Employer (EOE) and/or
nondiscrimination statement that explicitly includes gender identity and gender expression; equity, diversity, and inclusion as desired skills; and inclusive
questions about name, pronouns, and gender. None of these are deal break-
ers if absent—I do not necessarily pass on postings without them, primarily

because that would severely limit my options—but I am more enthusiastic about a place from the beginning when these elements are present.

Personal Experience

When I applied for librarian positions after graduate school, I came out as transgender in every interview. This was entirely my choice; it was my way of assessing how safe and comfortable I would feel at a place, as I did not want to have to hide my trans identity. For the most part, potential employers and coworkers did not respond badly. The most off-putting thing that was said to my face was someone asking what the pronouns I had listed on my CV meant, but that seemed to be lack of awareness rather than malice or bigotry. I did avoid places that I suspected would be less welcoming, so I cannot speak as to whether my experience would have been the same everywhere.

Legal Issues

There are some federal workplace protections for trans and gender variant people. Any business or institution that is an EOE—usually, any business with fifteen or more employees—is forbidden to "discriminate against a job applicant or an employee because of the person's race, color, religion, sex (including pregnancy, gender identity, and sexual orientation), national origin, age (40 or older), disability or genetic information" (U.S. Equal Employment Opportunity Commission, n.d.). A number of states, cities, and counties have additional employment and other protections specifically for trans and gender variant people; many, however, do not. Employers should familiarize themselves with any laws and protections that apply to them and use that information to support trans and gender variant applicants and employees.

EOE and Nondiscrimination Statements

As mentioned in the section above, most places with fifteen or more employees qualify as equal opportunity employers and are forbidden to discriminate for a variety of reasons, of which gender identity is one. For an applicant, however, simply knowing that is not the same as being confident that a potential employer takes it seriously. A very simple thing that employers can do is include an EOE statement in all job postings. When written to include all of the protected groups, this reminds both applicants and any employees involved in hiring that nondiscrimination is an important part of the process. In addition, many places have their own nondiscrimination statement; this may reiterate and/or be more comprehensive than the general language. Putting the statement in a job ad has a similar effect as posting the full EOE language. It also demonstrates that the institution has gone out of its way to create its own language, which affirms to applicants that nondiscrimination is a core value rather than just a legal requirement. Like so many other things, this is not solely an LGBTQ+ issue. Comprehensive EOE and nondiscrimination statements also inform people of color, people with disabilities, and anyone else worried about discrimination that they can expect protections during work as well as the application process.

Personal Experience

I have two examples from my most recent job search, which took place immediately after graduate school. One posting had the EOE statement at the bottom, but it was a limited version of it that listed sex but not orientation or gender identity. I do not think this was the only reason that I did not apply for the job, but it was a red flag. The Equal Opportunity Employment Commission has declared that gender identity is included under sex as a protected class; however, I did not know that at the time. Even now, that language would make me wary.

The other example is the position I ended up taking. The job posting simply tagged the abbreviation "EOE" on at the end. When serving on a search committee later, I found that the school actually has a really excellent nondiscrimination statement that includes, among other things, gender identity, gender expression, marital status, and sexual orientation. Seeing that on the job posting would have indicated what I quickly learned, that I would feel extremely well supported and comfortable being out there.

Gender-Neutral Language

When speaking or writing, always use *they/them/their/themself* for singular third-person pronouns when describing someone of unknown gender identity. In job descriptions, this includes people who use neutral pronouns by not assuming that the position will be filled by a male or female person. It is also much less awkward to write "they" instead of "he or she" every time. For more information, see Chapter 2, "Pronouns and Other Language."

Skills Requirement

An increasing number of libraries seem to be listing some form of equity, diversity, and/or inclusion (sometimes abbreviated to EDI) knowledge as a preferred or required skill on job postings. If done well, this serves several

> **" — "** **EXAMPLE LANGUAGE**
>
> "The successful candidate will start as soon as they are available."

purposes. It can indicate to trans and gender variant people (as well as others of marginalized identities) that the workplace actively values equity and inclusion; if that is indeed the case, it means a welcoming and supportive environment for trans and gender variant employees as well as patrons. It also creates space in the application and interview process for discussion of EDI in the context of the position. This allows applicants to share any work, training, or other relevant experiences. For the search committee, this discussion both shows them how the applicant thinks about EDI and provides an opportunity to talk about its role in the job, which is a selling point to some applicants. Remember that not everyone of a marginalized identity has experience or interest in EDI work. If this skill is part of the position or an expectation of the institution, it should be part of the application; the identity of the candidate has nothing to do with it.

Be specific. EDI is a huge, often poorly defined concept. When creating a job posting, think about what particular elements of it directly relate to the position and describe them. For example, "commitment to diversity" could mean almost anything, while "familiarity with accessibility standards," "Spanish language skills," and "racial equity training" are far more concrete. This helps qualified applicants know that their skills are a good fit for the position, which will make it more appealing to them. It also weeds out candidates without the necessary skills. In addition, library schools and professional organizations can more easily determine what professional development training to provide if employers are specific about what knowledge they want candidates to have. Do, however, allow for different types of experience. It may be tempting to make Safe Zone training required, but not everyone has access to it for free (if at all). Phrasing such as "Safe Zone training and/or relevant coursework and/or other experience with LGBTQ+ populations" shows what kind of experience the job requires while remaining open to people with a variety of backgrounds.

If the requirement is nonspecific, ask for more general information from applicants. Perhaps the job is flexible or does not focus on EDI skills day-to-day, but they are an important part of the library's mission and values. Whether through a question on a form, a cover letter, or an additional part of the application, ask candidates to write about their background in EDI. This is a way to learn something about the candidate that might be an asset to the position or the workplace as a whole but that might not come up otherwise. It also demonstrates to potential applicants that the organization takes EDI seriously and seeks people who are committed to it.

Ask for EDI skills only if they are part of the position and/or organizational values. This is not to say that you should not look for candidates who will bring the library skills that it lacks, but do so with intent and have a framework in place so that they are not expected to come in and shoulder all of the EDI work themselves. Without institutional and coworker support, change is extremely difficult and burnout comes quickly. This is even more the case when one's EDI work ties into aspects of one's own identity. Do not hire a trans or gender variant person with the expectation that they will automatically take on the labor of making your library more inclusive. Even if that is explicitly part or all of the job, do not expect them to do the work alone. Also, do not "diversify" your staff by hiring someone and then assume that any problems are fixed. Diversity comes as a result of successful inclusion work, not vice versa.

APPLICATIONS

Demographic Questions

Some employers are legally required to report demographic information on their applicants; this is why it is common to find a section or separate form on job applications asking about race and gender. This is often titled "Invitation to Self-Identify" or something similar. Supplying the information is completely optional, and skipping it has no effect on the rest of the application. Neither does filling it out, as answers should never be seen by the search committee or anyone else involved with the hiring process. The data is anonymized and reported to the Equal Employment Opportunity Commission (EEOC) and has no connection to individual applications or interviews.

This part of the application can be stressful for trans and gender variant people to fill out. Being asked about gender is rarely a good or easy thing. Not everyone is clear on how the demographic information gets used, so people may be concerned that outing themselves will damage their chances of being hired. Then there is the problem of the question itself. The overwhelming majority, in my experience, ask whether the applicant is male or female. This is problematic even for trans and gender variant people who do identify as one of these. Very few forms indicate whether they want legal gender or gender identity, thus completely failing to acknowledge that these may not be the same. Without a clear understanding of the purpose of the question and whether it affects the rest of the job application, trans and gender variant people may worry about the effects of an "incorrect" answer. On top of all of this, nonbinary people are rarely given an option that they identify with at all.

Fortunately, there are very easy ways to ask demographic questions inclusively. Specific information is collected by the EEOC, but the language on the form used to gather it is up to the employer. This means that the demographic forms do not need to erase trans and gender variant people even if the official data does. First, clearly state the purpose of the form. At the top (not in fine print at the bottom), tell applicants that it is entirely optional and has no bearing on the rest of their application. Make it clear that any information they provide will be anonymized and will never be shared with the search committee or anyone else involved with the hiring process. Second, ask gender identity. Reiterate that it is optional. Make this question fill-in-the-blank. Any multiple-choice version, however many options are listed, risks othering anyone who does not see themselves represented. Third, ask legal gender. Again, reiterate that it is optional. This one can be multiple-choice if necessary, but it should really be fill-in-the-blank as well. If multiple-choice, make sure that all applicable options are included (some states and countries have options in addition to male or female).

Names and Pronouns

Personal Experience

The name I was assigned at birth and used for about twenty-five years is a traditionally female one; most people attaching it to me would assume that I was female and used *she/her* pronouns. For a few years before coming out as trans, I adopted a neutral name that I was more comfortable with. During grad school, I started using my current name, which is a traditionally male one. For the first time, I looked into legally changing it. This was in large part because I knew I would be job hunting soon and wanted to avoid the difficulties that would come with using something other than my legal name. At the time, I lived in North Carolina, where the name change process takes months and a not-insignificant amount of money, so my first few job applications did have to go out with my original name on them. This was confusing for potential employers and deeply uncomfortable for me. Among other things, it meant that I had to find a way to out myself early in order to be called by my name of use. I was not sure what general practices were regarding what name I could use to apply for jobs; I often used my legal one because I did not want to risk missing an opportunity by not doing so. Some applications had a place for a preferred name or nickname, though that often did not get used by the systems or people following up on them. I tried a few different approaches, such as putting my name of use in parentheses at the top of CVs, but all of them required either leaving my legal name out (without knowing the potential repercussions when it came to background checks and such) or outing myself from the start. I did not object to potential employers knowing that I was trans, but being forced to share that information is invariably horrible whatever the reaction. My name change finally came through by the time I seriously started job hunting, which simplified everything greatly. The concern about background checks and past references (some of whom knew me by a previous name) remained, but that was manageable compared to the previous stresses.

There are several things to note about my experience. Clearly, I had no knowledge of whether one could simply put one's name of use on a job application or CV. I have since concluded that this is fine; one can share any relevant information when a potential employer declares their intention to run a background check. This still requires outing oneself, but it does not force it during the initial interview process. That said, I have gathered from a number of other job hunting trans and gender variant people that my concerns were not unique. A lot of us are not clear on what name to put on job applications if we do not use our legal one. Something else to remember about my story is that, while my experience may be very similar to that of many trans and gender variant people, it is in no way representative of everyone's. Some people may not ever change their legal name, by choice or otherwise. I always provide my pronouns in introductions, but by the time I was getting interviews most people assumed that I was a cisgender male, so misgendering was rare. This is not at all the case for plenty of trans and gender variant people; those who do transition physically may be pre- or mid-transition, while others, especially nonbinary people, may often have to out themselves or be consistently misgendered.

My intent in sharing this story is to give an example of how a lot of job applications can be extremely problematic for trans and gender variant people. Pronouns are similar to names of use in that it can be difficult to share them with potential employers without awkwardness and outing oneself. It is not at all difficult for employers to remove these difficulties completely; it just takes awareness and a little effort. Here are some ways to do that:

- If asking for a CV and/or cover letter, direct applicants to use whatever name they want you to call them. Perhaps mention that legal names may be asked for later for background checks.
- If asking applicants to fill out a form, specify legal name or name of use (even if only one of these is requested).
- Put an optional space for pronouns on all application forms. Make this fill-in-the-blank; even the most well-intentioned multiple-choice lists may leave someone out, which can be extremely othering. The optional nature of this is important; some people (even cisgender ones) may worry about damaging their chances at a position if they disclose gender identity, so never require them to do so. Pronouns are not the same as gender identity, but many people do not realize this and will assume that anyone using *he/him* pronouns is male.

> **❝ EXAMPLE LANGUAGE**
>
> "To apply, please email a cover letter and CV to human.resources@library.org. Use the name that you would like us to call you. We may request your legal name at a later point if it is needed."
>
> *On application forms:*
>
> Honorific (optional): _____
>
> Name of use*: _____
>
> Pronouns (optional): _____
>
> Current legal name: _____
>
> Past legal name(s) (optional): _____
>
> *Name of use* is what you want to be called in person and on written communications; this is what the search committee will see. Legal name(s) are used for background checks; Human Resources personnel will see this information, but it will not be shared with anyone else.

- If including a salutation field, include *Mx.* Usually pronounced "mix," this is the gender-neutral version of *Mr.* or *Ms.* As with the pronouns field, make it optional so that nobody is forced to disclose anything they do not want to.

As with the EOE statement, some libraries are not in charge of the language on application forms; this may be true for academic or state/county institutions where all hiring goes through devoted Human Resources departments. If this is the case, consider contacting that department and suggesting updates to the language. If the institution has an LGBTQ+ Center or something similar, try talking to them first; they may know if any similar efforts have been made and how best to proceed. It is also always worth asking them for feedback on inclusive hiring practices, as they will have specific knowledge about your institution and community.

INTERVIEWING

Names and Pronouns

As with applications, interviews can be stressful for some trans and gender variant people if there is not a comfortable way to share one's name of

Community Voices

From the interviewee side, I recommend being yourself. If you are attempting to "hide" and blend in as part of your everyday life, then continue to do so. If you post pro-trans information or before/after photos on Facebook, then leave it be. You do not want to appear as though you are being dishonest with a possible future employer. If you are out and proud it does not mean that you must announce your "transness" as part of your interview. Simply be yourself. If a library or institution rejects you because you are trans, you probably didn't want to work there anyway. Be thankful. If they know and accept you, you are in an excellent situation and one that you should continue to pursue.

If you are part of a hiring committee, you have a professional obligation to treat each candidate on their merits, not on their gender identity. Similar to not excluding candidates because they are men, or redheads, or have big noses—physical characteristics should not, and indeed cannot, come into play. Besides, eliminating a candidate because they are transgender means your bias may extinguish your best opportunity for a top-notch employee.

—Paige Flanagan

use and pronouns. By creating a space for this in the interview process, employers accomplish two things. First, they remove the stress of misgendering and judgment, which makes the interview itself much more comfortable for the applicant. Second, they tacitly inform the applicant that the workplace welcomes trans and gender variant people and has taken steps to make them feel welcome.

When contacting an applicant for an interview, ask what name and pronouns they would like you to use for them. The language here is important: never ask their gender identity or sex. This phrasing asks for no more than the name and pronouns they are comfortable with for the interview. Then make sure that everyone who meets with a candidate knows what name and pronouns to use. It is extremely disrespectful to misgender someone, especially after they have told you their pronouns. Always use the correct name and pronouns when discussing a candidate. There is no reason for anyone in the interview to use the candidate's legal name if that is not what they go by.

On your side, incorporate pronouns into every introduction session, regardless of the gender identity of the people involved. If at least some of the hosts state their pronouns, an applicant will not worry about confusing

> **"— EXAMPLE LANGUAGE**
> **—"**
>
> *For the candidate:*
>
> "We would like to schedule a phone interview with you to discuss the position. Which of the following times is best for you? Please also let us know what name and pronouns you would like us to use for you during the interview process."
>
> *For the search committee:*
>
> "This week we have phone interviews scheduled with Stephen Krueger (*he/him* or *they/them*), Padma Patil (*she/her*), and J. Alfred Prufrock (*ve/ver/vis*)."
>
> *During the interview:*
>
> "To start, we'll have the search committee introduce themselves. I'm Stephen Krueger, Access & Outreach Services Librarian. I use he/him or they/them pronouns."

people if they want to do the same. Often, trans and gender variant people are the only ones to provide their pronouns, which can implicitly out us. Normalizing pronoun sharing means that people do not have to out themselves in order to avoid misgendering. Nobody who feels uncomfortable doing so should feel obligated to share their pronouns. However, trans and gender variant people should not be the only ones to do so. Sharing pronouns may feel awkward at first, but it is an important step in normalizing trans and gender variant identities. See Chapter 2, "Pronouns and Other Language," for more information.

Restrooms

During a long in-person interview, it is likely that the candidate will ask where the restroom is at some point. As with patrons asking the same question, do not make assumptions about which one they prefer to use. Instead, provide options and leave them to decide which they are most comfortable with. This gives them information both about the workplace culture and the building's options, which may influence their decision about where to work. Do not comment on which restroom they use.

EXAMPLE LANGUAGE

"There is a men's room there, a women's room there, and an all-gender restroom there."

Health Insurance

If an interview includes a section on health insurance, make sure that whoever is in charge of that meeting is aware of the coverage for transition and other specific health needs. Do not bring it up in the meeting unless you do it with every candidate, but do be prepared to answer questions if someone has them. Some people may be uncomfortable asking in person, so provide candidates with ways to find out more on their own so that they do not have to out themselves to learn about coverage. You can do this by including information in whatever packet you give to candidates before or during interviews.

THE SEARCH COMMITTEE

Preparation

All of the suggestions in this chapter presuppose that your library is (or at least is trying to be) a gender-inclusive space. That means that everyone on the search committee should already have some knowledge of how to respectfully interact with trans and gender variant candidates. That said, you may want to remind them of best practices to make sure that everyone is on the same page. Before any phone or in-person interviews, go over a few things that may come up, such as pronoun sharing during introductions and how to give restroom directions inclusively (I was once asked by an interviewer what the pronouns on my CV meant, which was a red flag for me). Also prepare for questions about workplace climate, health insurance, and available resources for trans and gender variant employees, as how you answer these questions will tell the candidate a great deal about what to expect. Always be honest; even if you cannot provide an ideal response, you can demonstrate that you are aware of potential issues and have thought about gender inclusion in your workplace. You do not need to have done everything, but it goes a long way if you can demonstrate that you are working on it.

Bias and Transnegativity

Unfortunately, transphobia and bias are present in some library workers. Keep an eye out for these during the hiring process, as they may pop up in members of the search committee. Outright transphobia will probably be fairly obvious, and one would hope that enough people see and oppose it that it can be shut down quickly. If that is not the case, perhaps your library is not a safe place for a trans or gender variant person to work anyway; that is not remotely acceptable, obviously, and you should do everything possible to change it before any employees are harmed. Implicit bias is more complicated to pin down. Search committees often talk about "fit," which can be a red flag. To some extent, it is reasonable to assess how well someone will get along with potential coworkers. However, "fit" is vague enough to be an excuse when the real reason is discomfort with something about the candidate's identity. Language about "fitting in with the culture" can be used to reject people of marginalized identities. Focus on more concrete elements like skills and experience. When you consider other factors, encourage search committee members to be specific about what they do or do not like. You may find that someone backs down if pressed to define their own transnegative opinions; they may also not have realized the source of their own discomfort and change their perspective when they do. Perhaps you cannot change anyone's mind, but you can point out explicit or implicit bias when you see it.

CONCLUSION

Ultimately, the best way to make trans and gender variant applicants feel welcome is to maintain a supportive work environment. If your library has all-gender restrooms with good signage, candidates will notice them without your having to point them out. If pronoun sharing in group meetings is part of your library's culture, the search committee will not need to be reminded to do it. If all positions require some type of EDI work, that should show in the job description. The ideas in this chapter come naturally if the underlying values are present in the library's day-to-day practices. If that is not the case—if your library has not done the work necessary to support trans and gender variant employees—do not pretend otherwise in an attempt to get trans and gender variant people to come work for you. Do the labor first, or people will leave as soon as they can after finding out the truth. If you need help creating a gender-inclusive environment, hire someone to do that and be honest about the situation that they will be entering.

QUICK FIXES

- Make all language in job descriptions gender-neutral (unless referring to a person of known gender identity).
- Write out EOE statement in job postings.
- Include EDI questions in job postings, and follow up on them.
- Format demographic questions to include all identities.

- Give candidates the opportunity to tell you what name and pronouns to use for them before and during interviews (and pass that information on to everyone that they will interact with).
- Let visiting candidates know where all of the restrooms are.
- Remind members of search committees about gender-inclusive practices.
- Recognize and comment on bias in hiring processes.

LONG-TERM SOLUTIONS

- Create a gender-inclusive library so that all of this happens as part of general practice.

REFERENCE

U.S. Equal Employment Opportunity Commission. "About the EEOC: Overview." U.S. Equal Employment Opportunity Commission (accessed September 15, 2018), https://www.eeoc.gov/eeoc/.

6

Library Employees and Coworkers

This chapter discusses ways to encourage and support trans and gender variant people as employees and coworkers in the library, including sections on interviewing, transition at work, and student workers. It is an overview that delves into some library-specific situations. For more in-depth information, I recommend the excellent book *Transgender Employees in the Workplace: A Guide for Employers* (Kermode, 2017). Some of the content is specific to the United Kingdom, but much of it applies anywhere.

The previous chapter outlined some ways to make job postings and interviews more inclusive of trans and gender variant applicants. None of that means much, however, if the actual work environment is not equally inclusive. It is the responsibility of employers to make sure that all of their employees have the support they need, and it is the responsibility of everyone in a workplace to treat all of their coworkers with respect. It is not enough to assume that everyone means well and will get along. Some libraries may never have had a trans or gender variant employee, or at least not one who is out at work. Some library workers may never have had a trans or gender variant coworker that they know of. A lot of the difficult situations that trans and gender variant people run into at work are not caused by bigotry or malice, but are instead due to lack of awareness on the part of their employers or coworkers. However, this does not make the situations easier to deal with, so employers need to take active steps to resolve them (or, better still, preempt them). This chapter describes some ways in which libraries and their employees can support trans and gender variant people in the workplace. As always, listen to your own community first; do not prioritize anything in this book over the thoughts of any trans or gender variant people whom you work with.

A lot of the content of this chapter is addressed in more detail elsewhere in the book (such as restrooms and pronouns). I will talk about how these issues affect employees here, but see the other chapters for detailed best practices.

WHO DOES THE WORK?

In *Out Behind the Desk: Workplace Issues for LGBTQ Librarians*, K. R. Roberto (2011) acknowledges that trans librarians must often resign themselves to educating their coworkers on allyship, though this added labor perpetuates marginalization without disrupting the dominant group's privilege. In my experience, this is all too often true. Presumably you are reading this book because you care about making your library a place where people of all gender identities are treated equitably. It takes concrete time and labor to make this a reality. As you pursue this goal, pay attention to who ends up doing inclusion work and why.

Some trans and gender variant people may be able, willing, and happy to educate others about their identities and how best to support them. However, it should never be assumed that this is the case. EDI work can be extremely labor-intensive as well as emotionally draining, especially if one's own identity is directly involved. At best, it takes time and energy from someone's primary job (if that is different); it may also make them stressed and uncomfortable around their coworkers. For many trans and gender variant people, talking about issues like pronouns, health care, and restrooms means reliving unpleasant or traumatic experiences. That kind of emotional vulnerability and labor should never be expected of anyone unless they explicitly volunteer for it; even then, it should be handled very carefully by everyone involved.

Trans and gender variant library workers are obviously the ones most affected by ignorance about gender inclusion, but that does not make it our responsibility to educate others. We may end up doing so by choice or out of desperation, but there is a lot of time and emotional labor involved that can take away from our work. Educating and training others about our own identity is also extremely draining and can lead to burnout. In addition, doing it properly takes knowledge and experience; it does not come naturally just because of someone's gender identity.

With all that in mind, no trans or gender variant employee should be expected to do any more gender inclusion work than a cisgender person in a comparable position. That is to say, everyone has the basic human responsibility to treat other people with respect, and it would be best if everyone's job involved some type of inclusion work, but the active labor beyond that should not be forced only on people of marginalized identities. This means that it should be explicitly part of one or more positions. If it is not, those most affected may end up taking it on because otherwise it will not happen at all, and they are the ones who will be harmed.

EDI Positions and Committees

There are an increasing number of positions focused on equity and inclusion. This is excellent! It means that libraries are realizing that they need to actively channel resources into countering a history and culture of exclusion, segregation, and inaccessibility. Titles, duties, and requirements vary widely, as they should, to suit the specific needs of the library and community. Institutions that have or create positions like these also have a responsibility to support the people who fill them. In addition to the usual ways of supporting employees, this includes making sure that they are able to do their work effectively. It is not enough to hire someone and expect them to make a library more inclusive on their own. Other employees must be made aware of the new position and what it entails, so that they react appropriately when approached with recommended changes and new ideas.

Even if your library does not have a designated position like this, you can create a committee to do similar work. It may be tempting to ask any out LGBTQ+ people to participate, but this is tokenizing and possibly ineffective; being trans does not automatically make someone knowledgeable about gender inclusion (the same goes for race, disability, and any other marginalized identity). If you handpick members of such a committee, make them people who are actually interested in EDI work. There may be overlap (a lot of the people studying gender inclusion are trans or gender variant), but focus on work, scholarship, or interest instead of identity.

 Community Voices

As a manager, department head, associate professor, whatever, you have power. In institutions we have power to hire/retain/fire people and foster relationships, initiate/ change/end projects, change policies, and set examples through our behavior.

Power dynamics underlie all systems of oppression and once you see them, you can't unsee them. Be ready to find areas where you aren't aware of power dynamics yet. When you become a manager or take on a leadership role you now have leadership powers like legitimate power, coercive power, and referent power, to name a few. You must acknowledge and work with them.

Tips for managers of people who are doing diversity work:

- ***Document it.*** *Diversity work sometimes doesn't have written evidence, so create it! Ask employees to write their diversity work into their work plans and include it in their evaluations. Written communications boost tenure dossiers, and any external documentation of uncompensated/"extra" labor adds validity. Write thank you letters for achievements on organizational letterhead. Become an expert at tedious paperwork and describing the value of your folks' work.*

- **Talk about it.** *Giving your employees credit in public spaces boosts their morale and lets everyone else know that they're doing the work, and that it's important. Talking about it with your supervisors and peers shows other managers that it's something that's important.*
- **Sit down.** *Refer or delegate opportunities for participation, presentation, publishing, and so on (while also keeping in mind that many folks doing diversity work are probably overtaxed). You're a manager, and others need a chance.*
- **Reach back.** *Do the things you couldn't do before when you weren't in a position of power. Find mentorship opportunities, donate, spend time helping others reach their goals.*
- **Change policy, not hearts and minds.** *Work to create a workplace that doesn't just accommodate folks who are different, but that actively works to affirm them. Use your positionality to advocate for structural change. Actively engage with your organization's hiring processes and personnel policies and read up on how those processes can be improved.*
- **Network aggressively.** *Your position gets you more and different types of contacts. Make it your job to learn about existing experts and resources at your institution that could be good connections for organization-wide work.*
- **Listen.** *If your employee is bringing something to you, they are doing it for a reason. What should you do with it, who else needs to know about it, how can you help, and how can you amplify the work?*
- **Communicate.** *Informational power is now one of your superpowers. Your job as a manager is to share information.*
- **Make space.** *Create as much flexibility as you can for folks. Trust them, even if you don't understand their point of view. If it seems that they are struggling, ask if they are interested in finding a mentor outside of your department or organization. Ask them what they need. Follow up.*
  —Erin White, Virginia Commonwealth University Libraries

TRAINING EMPLOYEES

General Education

While some library employees may bring their own experience and knowledge about inclusive practices, this cannot be assumed to be the case for everyone. It is the responsibility of the employer to make sure that everyone has at least the training necessary to practice whatever policies of inclusion the library has. Start with Safe Zone training or something similar; this provides attendees with general information on LGBTQ+ identities and some of the challenges we face. Contact your campus or local LGBTQ+ Center or equivalent, if one exists; they may offer trainings or know where you can find a trainer. Gender inclusion training can be more difficult to find, but that is a good idea if it is possible. The needs and experiences of trans and gender variant people sometimes overlap but are often very different from those of other LGBTQ+ people, so it is valuable to devote time to those identities in particular. Both Safe Zone and gender inclusion trainings are important because they ensure at least a basic level of knowledge; they also partly remove the burden of educating others from your LGBTQ+ employees.

All library employees, ideally including security and volunteers, should participate, as everyone interacts with LGBTQ+ patrons and coworkers (if anyone argues that this is not relevant to their work, it is probably an indicator that they need it most). If you are a particularly small library and cannot afford the cost on your own, reach out to other departments or local businesses and see if people want to participate in a combined training. Some organizations or individuals offer train-the-trainer sessions; send employees to this if you get the chance, as then you will have someone in-house who can work with other library staff as needed. Because of the ongoing changes in how people express their identities, offer the trainings at least every few years to avoid outdated information; this also ensures that new employees do not miss them.

When you offer these general trainings for your employees, you must arrange it so that everyone can attend. This may require flexibility in scheduling or offering multiple sessions. If you schedule them outside of work hours, compensate attendees accordingly. If you need to travel to a different location, make sure that everyone has a way to get there. Research any models you have for other required training, such as workplace safety or Title IX, and see if you can adapt that. If there is no way for all employees to attend (such as if you cannot afford multiple sessions and need the library to remain open while they happen), supply any who cannot attend with print or digital versions of the information. It is a good idea to have informal follow-up discussions, especially if you attended a session that was not just for the library. Here, your employees can share their thoughts and ask questions if they did not feel comfortable doing so before. This is also a good way for anyone who missed the training to catch up.

Library Practices

After all of your employees have undergone general training, they should learn about how it applies to their work. This is much easier to do logistically, as it probably is best to do within departments. This is because specific best practices for gender inclusion vary widely based on what one's job is. Think of Safe Zone or gender inclusion training as teaching your employees *why* this is important; it is then your responsibility to teach them *how* to do it in the workplace. Use the information in this book to decide what gender inclusion looks like in your department, then train your employees to practice it.

Some employees may be resistant to adopting gender-inclusive practices. This often comes from ignorance and discomfort with new concepts, which can be resolved through education. Make sure that any group trainings and discussions are designed to invite questions. All participants should be discouraged from judging others for exposing ignorance, as this will increase discomfort with the topic. If you are more familiar with gender inclusion than your coworkers, you can invite people to talk to you individually if they do not want to ask something in front of a group. Also provide resources for them to explore on their own.

Resistance may also stem from personal opinions and beliefs. Ignorance about trans and gender variant people may be a related factor, but it can be more difficult to address in these situations. Focusing on the reasons behind intentional transnegativity may hurt your cause rather than help it, as people rarely respond well to perceived attacks on their beliefs. Instead, make the issue about treating patrons and coworkers respectfully. You cannot tell an employee what to think, but you can require certain behavior in the workplace. This is one reason that gender inclusion policies are so important: they standardize best practices instead of leaving them up to individual employees. See Chapter 8, "Patron Complaints and Employee Objections," for guidelines on how to react to a specific concern.

NAMES AND PRONOUNS

This information has been comprehensively covered in other chapters, and it may seem repetitive. That is because for people who are regularly misgendered, it comes up almost every time they meet a new person. Learning and correctly using coworkers' names and pronouns is one of the most basic ways to treat trans and gender variant people with respect. Misgendering people is always rude and creates a toxic work environment. If power dynamics are added to the mix, misgendering people becomes even more harmful; in addition to putting the misgendered person in the position of having to correct a superior or tolerate the disrespect, it sets an example to other employees that misgendering is acceptable.

The simplest way to learn a coworker's pronouns, if they want to share them, is to offer your own when you introduce yourself. This way, you are demonstrating that you are open to hearing theirs without demanding that they share. Do this regardless of your own gender identity or whether you

Community Voices

I've been gender nonconforming since adolescence so that was clear when I was hired for my first library assistant position. However, over the five years that I worked there I became more visibly gender nonconforming and eventually came out as transgender.

At a certain point my supervisor (the library director) began to see this as a threat. I was shouted at in front of coworkers and formally reprimanded twice, once for suggesting a technique to help coworkers use my correct pronouns. My supervisor made no attempt to use the correct pronouns, even commenting one year after I came out that everyone needed more time to adjust to the change.

Unfortunately, because it was a small library with only three full-time staff members including myself and the director, there was no one I could go to for mediation or resolution. After I left, my supervisor continued to harass me on social media for several weeks. Although my state has explicit coverage for gender identity and expression in its nondiscrimination law, I didn't have enough money to hire a lawyer so I felt it was safest to leave even though I didn't have another job lined up. Thankfully I was offered my current job while I was in the process of leaving, but it has damaged my confidence and left gaps in my recommendation history.

If there were some national- or state-level grievance, accountability, or mediation body it might have made a difference in how my supervisor handled her discomfort. Because I was speaking "up" a power differential to assert my rights, I was accused of insubordination. An outside body tasked with reminding library managers of their legal duties and the ethical standards of the profession in the absence of internal resources might have made a difference in how I was treated. At the very least it could have enforced even nominal or reputational consequences for her illegal treatment of me as a gender nonconforming trans man and simultaneous, unrelated bigoted treatment of library patrons.

—Loren R. Klein

think your pronouns are obvious. The purpose is normalization so that those people who want or need to share their pronouns can do so without singling themselves out. Do not be surprised or offended if other people do not share their pronouns, and do not feel obligated to share yours if you prefer not to do so.

EXAMPLE LANGUAGE

"I'm Stephen, the Access & Outreach Services Librarian. My pronouns are he/him or they/them."

In addition to individual introductions, there are a number of ways to normalize workplace pronoun sharing. If you are in a position to determine the template for email signatures, nametags, and business cards, add an optional pronoun field. This makes it easy for anyone to include their pronouns, and it lets everyone know that it is a standard workplace practice. If you ever lead meetings, incorporate pronouns into group introductions there (see Chapter 2, "Pronouns and Other Language," for examples of how to do this). In both of these situations, be aware that some people may not understand what to do or why; provide some explanation and invite people to come to you with any questions.

RESTROOMS

All-gender restrooms for patrons are becoming more common in libraries, but employee access sometimes gets forgotten. It is extremely important that everyone feels safe and comfortable using the restroom in their workplace. In many situations where people are harassed and misgendered in restrooms, they at least do not have to worry about meeting the harasser again; if this happens in the workplace, they may have to regularly interact. Even if other employees are supportive, this can create an immensely stressful and toxic work environment. To preempt this, make it clear that your library's gender-inclusive restroom policy applies to employees as well, and educate all staff on what it means. Whatever your position, never question a coworker's presence in a restroom. See Chapter 4, "Restrooms," for guidelines on how to provide everyone with options that they can comfortably use, and make sure that employee restrooms follow the same standards. If this is not already the case, make it a goal to offer accessible, all-gender restrooms that employees can easily get to.

HEALTH INSURANCE

The health insurance available to library employees is often outside of their direct control; a government or institutional department may determine the policies. This does not mean that managers, supervisors, and directors have no responsibility to their employees when it comes to this area. Health insurance can have a huge influence on the quality of life for some trans and gender variant people, as it often determines one's ability to physically transition. If you have any control over the health insurance provided to your employees, educate yourself on whether it covers transition-related costs; if it does not, do everything in your power to change that. Even if you are not directly in charge of health insurance, communicate with whoever is and try to improve coverage for trans and gender variant employees. Do not wait until someone asks you about it; trans and gender variant people should not have to out themselves or share their medical needs with employers to have those needs covered.

Personal Experience

When I started my current position, I was unsure whether my new health insurance covered hormone therapy and other transition-related costs. Through some miscommunication with the pharmacy I had generally concluded that it did not. Finding out for certain was on my list of things to do at some point, but it involved going to the college's human resources office and talking about my gender identity and transition; even if the conversation went well, it would be stressful, so I was putting it off. At some point I casually mentioned the issue to my supervisor, who (without my having asked and without mentioning me by name) contacted the relevant department and reported back. The information itself was that the coverage was actually excellent, but what I remember most was how supported I felt by my supervisor's actions. The barriers that had prevented me from finding the information I needed (lack of knowledge about whom to ask, concern about the reaction, stress of talking about my identity to strangers) simply did not exist for her (a cisgender woman and longtime employee, who could ask from her position as supervisor instead of focusing on an individual employee), and she used that power to remove the barriers for me. I cannot think of a better example of allyship from someone in a leadership position.

TRANSITION AT WORK

In general, trans and gender variant people should not have to out themselves to be respected at work. However, the process of transitioning usually does require coming out if one wants to be called by the correct name and pronouns. Employees on almost every level can take steps to make coworkers' transition less stressful, at least in the workplace.

Employee names show up in all sorts of places that are outside of their control, from library directories to ILS accounts to email addresses. All of these should default to the person's name of use (unless it is absolutely necessary to use their legal one, such as on tax documents). When someone

Community Voices

I have presented as gender nonconforming my entire professional career. I was That Confident Butch who wore suits and wingtips, stating my she/they pronouns in meetings, and generally being open and willing to answer questions. Even though I knew that by my very existence, my presentation, I was in a constant state of outing myself, it didn't bug me. I was visible, but I was visible in a way I was comfortable with.

When I realized that no, I wasn't just a masculine woman but a transmasculine nonbinary person, it suddenly wasn't comfortable. It wasn't like in college when I could experiment and change on a dime. Now I had to give my new name and pronouns in meetings. I had to correct people in front of entire departments. I had to not freeze when my deadname was displayed to students during instruction sessions.

I feel lucky to work in an organization where the bureaucratic element of transitioning isn't too bad. But it's the loaded "I go by Jay now, and please use they pronouns" conversations that are draining. It's the "how do I deal with my previous publications." It's having such a personal change become public to my entire profession.

—Jay L. Colbert

changes either their name of use or their legal name, make sure the change is reflected everywhere without their having to request it specifically. If this takes time, let them know that it may be a few days (or whatever) before the change shows up but that it will happen. Do not wait until an employee transitions to work out how name changes should work. Instead, have a procedure in place. One may already exist, as many people change their names after marriage, but make sure that all relevant employees know how to apply it when someone transitions.

Never demonstrate frustration when someone's transition requires work on your part. Is it inconvenient to change an employee's email address or to learn new pronouns? Possibly, but I guarantee that they are far more stressed about it than you are. Expressing irritation, even if you mean to direct it at yourself or the system rather than the individual, can make the person feel that their transition is an unwelcome burden. This can lead to shame and hesitation to approach you for transition-related needs.

I have said this before, but it is especially important when a coworker is transitioning: never question anyone's presence in a restroom. If someone starts using a different restroom than they previously have, do not act surprised or comment. Call no attention to it, even affirmatively, unless they raise the subject (explicitly and verbally, not just by their presence). Interact with them precisely as you would anyone else using any restroom. Do the same if they choose not to change which restroom they use.

When a coworker transitions, all you need to know is how to refer to them. If you are unsure, ask privately what name and pronouns they would like you to use. Do not ask for any further information about their transition. They may choose to tell you how they identify or share other information about their experiences, but only discuss this if they raise the subject first. Most of all, never ask about anyone's physical transition. Also do not demand that they answer your questions about trans people in general. It is fine if they do want to talk about any of this, but pressuring them to satisfy your curiosity is extremely rude and can create an uncomfortable work environment. Simply learn the correct name and pronouns and use them. For specific guidelines, including what to do if you accidentally misgender someone, see Chapter 2, "Pronouns and Other Language."

SUPPORTIVE BEHAVIOR

A lot of the information in this chapter is geared toward managers and others with the power to create and enforce policy and practice. However, the day-to-day behavior of employees is an enormous factor in whether trans and gender variant people feel comfortable at work. As an individual, you can do a number of things to make this happen.

First, eliminate your own transnegative behavior. Even if you do not mean to, you may inadvertently do things that make trans or gender variant coworkers uncomfortable. Do not assume or expect that they will tell you if this is the case; especially if they do not know you well, they have no way of telling what your intent may be. It is your responsibility to assess your

Community Voices

My coworkers are my family. I was open with them about being a trans man when I first got hired, and ever since they have found ways to support and validate my identity. Working directly with the public—in the same small town I grew up in, no less—I am often misgendered by patrons. It's embarrassing and mentally exhausting when I have to correct someone on my pronouns, so it's nice to have that reprieve with my coworkers. In fact, they make it a point to emphasize my correct gender in front of certain patrons who haven't quite gotten the message. It shows just how much they care about me, and for that I am truly grateful to my work family.

—Devin Spencer, they/them or he/him, Library Assistant II

own behavior and think about how it comes across to others. Here are some general ways to stop your own transnegative behavior:

- Do not assume gender identity: You cannot tell someone's gender identity by their appearance, voice, name, or any other way unless they explicitly tell you. Do not make assumptions about a coworker's gender identity based on any of these things.

- Do not misgender people: Use the name, pronouns, and terminology that someone has asked you to use for them, whether they are present or not. Do not question them or anyone else about why they use that language.

- Do not restroom police: Never tell or imply to a coworker that they are in the wrong restroom.

- Eliminate the gender binary: Avoid creating gendered social events, dress codes, and other things that erase the existence of nonbinary people.

- Minimize gendered language: Unless you explicitly know the gender identity of everyone involved, avoid language like "ladies and gentlemen," "girls," or other gendered terms; if the words do not apply to everyone there, you end up misgendering people.

It is not enough to eliminate transnegative behavior. Because of the cisnormative nature of so many workplaces and other environments, trans and gender variant people cannot assume that a group or individual respects and supports their gender identity without active affirmation. This is why actions such as pronoun sharing, which may seem unnecessary to you, are so important; even if people correctly assume your gender identity, sharing your pronouns demonstrates that you understand the importance of asking rather than assuming gender identity. If a coworker transitions or otherwise comes out to you, find ways to affirm to them that you are not going to reject them because of it. Perhaps you can make sure they are invited on lunch trips to the dining hall; perhaps you stop by their desk occasionally to share pictures of your cats. Friendly behavior that does not mention gender identity is an important way to help trans and gender variant people feel supported at work. Make it clear that you value them as a person in ways unrelated to their gender. If a coworker changes the name and pronouns they use at work, affirm that you will do your best and that you will not be upset if they correct you when you make mistakes. This is also a good time to ask if they want you to correct others.

It is admirable to want to be a trans ally. However, this is not something you can simply decide to be. Allyship is expressed through ongoing actions, not self-centered declarations, and it takes work. If you want trans and gender variant people to trust you, do the labor of creating a safe environment so that they do not have to. Remember that it is not entirely up to you whether someone feels comfortable around you; past experiences with others, or aspects of your own behavior, may make some trans and gender

EXAMPLE LANGUAGE

"I saw the email HR sent about your name and pronouns. That's great; I'm so glad you feel comfortable enough to be out here. Please feel free to correct me if I make mistakes—I want to make sure I'm referring to you properly. Also, would you like me to correct other people on your behalf if I overhear any mistakes, or should I keep quiet?"

variant people unwilling to come out to you, and you have no right to expect anyone to do so.

CONCLUSION

I recognize that this chapter has been a little all over the place. This is because there is no one simple way to make sure that your trans and gender variant employees and coworkers feel supported. The ways in which gender identity can affect one's work life are myriad and often invisible to people who have not had similar experiences. As demonstrated in this chapter, everything from nametags to workplace restroom options to health insurance to committee assignments can be an avenue for stress or support, depending on how each situation is managed by those in power. Interpersonal interactions are more difficult to quantify but can be even more influential in one's happiness, or even feeling of safety, in the workplace. It is not the responsibility of trans and gender variant people to educate their coworkers and supervisors; conversely, it is up to everyone in a workplace to treat the people around them with respect.

QUICK FIXES

- Share your own pronouns when meeting new coworkers and in other introductions, if you are comfortable doing so.
- Add optional pronoun fields to employee templates (nametags, email signatures, business cards, etc.).
- Support coworkers when they transition and/or come out to you (by treating them as people, not by focusing on their gender).

LONG-TERM SOLUTIONS

- Require Safe Zone or other LGBTQ+ training for all employees, especially managers/supervisors.
- Train employees in specific gender inclusion practices for their positions.

- Provide trans-inclusive health insurance for employees.
- Provide accessible all-gender restrooms for library employees.
- Identify and eliminate your own transnegative assumptions and behavior.

REFERENCES

Kermode, Jennie. *Transgender Employees in the Workplace: A Guide for Employers.*
   London: Jessica Kingsley, 2017.
Roberto, K. R. "Passing Tips and Pronoun Police: A Guide to Transitioning at Your
   Local Library." In *Out Behind the Desk: Workplace Issues for LGBTQ Librari-
   ans*, edited by T. M. Nectoux, 121–127. Duluth, MN: Library Juice Press, 2011.

7

Conferences and Other Events

A note on authority: I have never organized a library conference or similar event, so the suggestions here are based on my observations as an attendee and on conversations with people who have done the planning work. They are by no means comprehensive or universally applicable. If the particulars do not apply to you, develop your own ways to achieve the goal of making your event gender inclusive.

However prepared one imagines oneself to be for an event, there are always unanticipated situations that come to light only when the first trans or gender variant person attends. Even that is not entirely correct: it must be a person who is willing to say something to the organizers if they find a problem, which often means drawing uncomfortable focus to their gender identity or outing themselves if they aren't already. It is impossible to know for certain, but I usually assume that anything that causes a complaint has already affected any number of people who did not want, or did not know how, to bring it up. This may be exacerbated for conferences, workshops, and other similar events. Attendees may not feel enough possession of the space to speak up; they may choose to simply tolerate a situation that happens once a year or less that they would not if it were part of their day-to-day work. It is also easy to simply not attend an event that makes one uncomfortable rather than take on the stress of trying to change it. Therefore, it is the responsibility of those organizing the event to make sure that people of all genders will be equitably treated there. This chapter provides some guidelines for doing so.

BEFORE THE EVENT

Many organizations have a diversity committee or equivalent; some may have a specific LGBTQ+ group (such as ALA's Gay, Lesbian, Bisexual, and Transgender Round Table). If you are on a planning committee for an event, invite this group to offer suggestions on how to make it more gender inclusive. The response will likely be positive, especially if the group is sponsoring presentations or is otherwise already involved. If the event location has a group that knows the space, such as a campus LGBTQ+ Center or equivalent, reach out to them to ask for advice as well; they may have specific local information that will help. Establishing these connections will help preempt potential issues, and it will also make handling problems easier when they do arise. Write this practice into whatever event planning guidelines you use so that it happens every time and is not dependent on one person thinking of it after the planning committee changes.

Develop a gender inclusion policy for your organization's events. It does not have to be overly specific; the purpose is to be the basis for the practices outlined in the rest of this chapter. If a policy already exists, review it to make sure the content and terminology are current. Ask the groups described above to look it over as well.

You can seek individual input, but be careful how you ask. As always, do not expect someone to help based purely on their identity (that is, do not expect a trans coworker to take on the labor if they are not otherwise involved). Also do not assume that people will bring their concerns to you if you have not made it clear that you want to hear them. Someone may have something to say but not know whom to contact; they may also have concerns about outing themselves by speaking up. You can, however, create avenues for input so that anyone who does want to offer it feels welcome to do so. If you are working with one of the specialized groups mentioned above, see if they want to reach out to their members or have other ideas. An anonymous survey is a good way to make sure people feel safe telling you their thoughts, and those who are comfortable can include their contact

 EXAMPLE LANGUAGE

Seeking individual feedback:

"We would like to make sure that people of all gender identities feel welcome at this event. If you want to share any thoughts or suggestions for doing this successfully, please fill out this survey."

Reaching out to LGBTQ+ centers or other local groups:

"We will be holding a conference at [location]. Do you have any suggestions for making it gender inclusive? Is there anything in particular we should know about the location?"

information for further discussion there; you can share this by emailing organization members and putting the link on the event registration form.

If you seek input from groups or individuals, be prepared to act on it. Seriously consider all suggestions, even if they are not what you want to hear. Remember that your event is almost certainly starting from a place of cisnormativity, so it will take additional work and funding to make it fully gender inclusive. Asking for input without intending to take action can seem tokenizing and alienating to the people who take the time to respond. If you do not have time to change something immediately, announce plans to do so in future.

LOCATION

Repercussions of Transnegative Locations

It is possible for the location of an event to be inherently transnegative. Perhaps it is a state that has explicitly or implicitly passed antitrans legislation; perhaps it is an institution that is known to discriminate against trans and gender variant people. Regardless of how inclusive the event attempts to be, these factors can make trans and gender variant people feel unsafe or uncomfortable simply being there.

Personal Experience

There was a small library event not too long ago that sticks in my mind. It was the annual meeting of a state interest group for a topic that I am very much involved in, and I was excited to go until the location was announced. That year's meeting was hosted by a religious university notorious for discriminating against LGBTQ+ students and employees, especially trans people. I briefly wrestled with that information, as I did very much want to attend the meeting. There was really no question, though. The prospect of setting foot there made my skin crawl. I ultimately emailed the person who had let me know about the meeting and said that I was unwilling to attend any events at the hosting school due to their treatment of trans people. My intent hadn't been to start anything more than an awareness of the issue, but I was pleasantly surprised when several others (some LGBTQ+, some not) joined my tiny boycott.

There are a lot of messages that can be drawn from the story above, and I am going to spend some time unpacking them to show the harm done by something as seemingly straightforward as the location of an event.

1. *Immediate loss of opportunity to the individual:* Passing on a professional development opportunity may mean missing out on connections and experience that would otherwise benefit one's work and career. The people most likely to feel unwelcome or unsafe are those already underrepresented in the profession (LGBTQ+ people, people of color, people with disabilities), and this type of situation adds yet another barrier. This can be especially harmful to those new to the profession who need the development opportunities and do not yet have the connections to safely express their concerns.

2. *Long-term discomfort or lack of trust:* Knowing that a group or organization does not support you can be a powerful deterrent to future participation. A person may choose a different area of work, or even a different career path, if they cannot expect to safely and comfortably attend the same events that others in their field can.

3. *Lower quality of work:* This affects both marginalized individuals and the group as a whole. Even if one is required or feels obligated to attend an event, discomfort and lack of trust in the group make it very difficult to do high-quality work. A person who feels unwelcome might, through no fault of their own, be unable to demonstrate their abilities and knowledge to potential colleagues; the group also loses out on what they might have done if they had felt more comfortable.

4. *Limiting diversity in the profession:* Libraries have an extensive history of segregation, inaccessibility, and exclusion. This is perpetuated by events that keep traditionally marginalized people from comfortably participating or exclude them entirely. At best, this keeps members of these groups from having the same opportunities in library work as the white, cisgender, heterosexual, abled people who make up so much of the profession. At worst, they will simply leave and find another career that treats them equitably.

Selecting a Location

Anyone involved in the location selection process, including third-party facilitators as well as all members of the planning committee, should be made aware that gender inclusion is an important factor. Having a written gender inclusion policy for events is a good way to make sure this does not depend on word-of-mouth and is not considered optional. The policy can serve as the basis for writing specific gender-inclusive practices, such as all-gender restrooms, into contracts with hosting facilities.

In an ideal world, it would be easy to simply eliminate any venue that did not meet the standards for gender inclusion. However, this may not always be the case, especially with large events. Requirements such as size, cost, availability, accessibility, and other logistics can severely limit choice of location. For smaller meetings, hosting may rotate between member institutions or go to whoever volunteers that year; refusing to let one member host may damage relationships as well as requiring someone else to take on the responsibility and labor. In all of these situations, having a gender inclusion policy for the organization is a good first step; potential venues can be asked how how they plan to abide by it and what steps they will take to counter transnegative factors. All-gender restrooms, inclusive registration and nametags, dress codes, and the other specific best practices described in this chapter are always important, but in this case they are another way to demonstrate that the organization prioritizes inclusion even if the location does not.

In general, clear communication with membership about parts of the process may help avoid confusion. This is especially important if a transnegative place is chosen. Without explanation, all that potential attendees know is that antitrans policies (or whatever the issue is) were not a deterrent for the organization. For me, this usually means I do not attend the event and may stop any participation with the group. If the issue is acknowledged and the decision explained, trans and gender variant people at least know that their concerns were considered. They may still choose not to attend (this would probably be my choice), but they may not feel as ignored and rejected by the organization.

To be clear, a gender-inclusive venue should always be the choice if one is available. There are some things that can be done if not, but none of them can fully counter the discomfort or fear that trans and gender variant people experience when forced to go to a place that does not respect our humanity. If you must use a transnegative location for your event, use the experience as motivation to avoid doing so in future.

If a Location Cannot Be Moved

Because large conferences are often scheduled years in advance, a location may become transnegative after it has been selected, when it is too late to choose another. You may have a policy against meeting in states with anti-trans legislation, but what if a new law is passed after you have committed and paid for the space? The section above has some guidelines for when you do end up using a transnegative space, and those apply here as well: active work to make the event itself gender inclusive, coupled with transparency about the decision to stay and how the organization will make sure all attendees feel comfortable.

Even so, be prepared for some trans and gender variant people and those who support us to stay away. This may be a personal decision based on principle, solidarity, or legitimate fear for one's safety. There are also some institutions (the state of California, most famously) that do not fund travel to states with anti-LGBTQ+ legislation, so employees of those places would have to pay their own way to attend. Whatever the reason, do not shame anyone for skipping, and do not try to explain away their concerns.

Boycotting

As an attendee, you have the option to boycott events in transnegative locations. If you do this, let the organizers know why you are staying away so they are aware of the effects of the location on attendance. If you are comfortable doing so, also let other people know; there may be attendees who are not aware of the issue who will act on the information in their own ways. Sometimes all it takes is one person willing to speak up; those who have not been sure how to express their support will then have some direction for doing so. If you are a cisgender person who is not personally affected, still consider joining boycotts or otherwise telling event organizers that you value gender inclusion.

Whatever you choose to do, do not shame anyone for making a different decision. Some people will suffer professionally if they do not attend an event. A lot of professional committees require conference attendance, and presenting at conferences is one of the main ways that library workers develop professionally. Attending a transnegative event does not mean that someone does not support trans and gender variant people or that they are comfortable being there.

RESTROOMS

There is a full chapter on restrooms earlier in this book, but there are also some specific situations that apply to conferences and other special events. If you are involved in planning an event, make sure that equitable options are provided for people of all gender identities. The first step is to create an inclusive restroom policy (see Chapter 4, "Restrooms," for guidelines). This should be made publicly available on the conference website, app, and manual, as well as posted by the restrooms themselves.

What restrooms are already provided at the location? Consider the current all-gender options. Are they as prominently available as the gendered restrooms, or do people need to go further out of their way to use them? Are they accessible to people with disabilities? Are there any other barriers that make them more difficult to use than the gendered options? If so, or if there are no all-gender restrooms available, convert some of the others for the duration of the event. To do this, simply cover the existing signage. Also make sure to note restroom options and locations in any conference directories and on-site signage (the last conference I attended did have some available, but they were out of the way enough that I did not stumble across them until the very end when someone pointed them out).

All restroom signage should be clear and readable from a distance. I remember a recent large conference where the all-gender restroom signs consisted of the organization logo and a block of text explaining the purpose

Community Voices

After grabbing my badge at the 2018 American Library Association's Annual Conference in New Orleans, I consulted the conference app to find the nearest gender-neutral restroom. I traversed the cavernous convention center to the appointed restroom, which had been converted from "women's" to "gender neutral." As I approached, a convention center employee waved me away, saying I could not use that restroom. As they spoke, I continued to advance, and once they decided I am a woman (I'm not), they apologized and welcomed me in.

I started to sweat as other conference goers noticed the interaction. I pointed out that the sign behind this employee read that the bathroom was available to everyone. They let me know that their manager was uncomfortable with gender-neutral bathrooms and had vetoed the ALA.

I felt angry and humiliated, especially since I was there to present on the first-ever all-trans ALA panel. By the time my ensuing tweet gained some attention, the situation was "fixed," but I wish ALA would have been, and would be, more proactive and progressive in preventing this experience. The knowledge that I was markedly unsafe at a gathering of my own profession hung over me for the rest of my trip.

—Ray Lockman, they/them/their, librarian

of all-gender restrooms and how one should behave in them. While presumably well intentioned, this made the restrooms very difficult to find; one had to be within a few yards to understand what the signage meant at all. A simple toilet logo with the text "All-Gender Restroom" would have been far more effective. It is not a bad idea to post an explanation or restroom policy beside that, but they should not replace the recognizable symbol.

An easily forgotten element of restroom planning is coordination with the on-site staff. At the incident described in the Community Voices section above, the organization had relabeled some central multistall restrooms as all-gender, but employees of the convention center had taken it upon themselves to prevent some people from using them. Staff education is always an important step when adding all-gender restrooms, and temporary events are no exception. When you create a restroom policy for a conference, make sure that it is shared with any staff who will be there in advance of the event so they can be trained to respect it.

EXAMPLE LANGUAGE

Gender-inclusive restroom policy:

"All attendees of [organization]'s events are encouraged to use the restroom that best corresponds to their gender identity (for example, the men's or the all-gender restroom for a person identifying as male). The decision of which to use should be left up to the individual. Event staff, including on-site employees, will be educated in the meaning and application of this policy before events begin."

Signage (to be placed outside each restroom):

"All attendees of [event] are encouraged to use the restroom that best corresponds with their gender identity." [Include map or list of restroom options]

Communicating with on-site staff:

"[Organization] has a gender-inclusive restroom policy. This means that some of the restrooms will be designated all-gender for the duration of the conference and that everyone is encouraged to use whichever space best corresponds with their gender identity. Please review the policy with all event staff before the conference begins. If you have any questions about this, please contact [contact]."

REGISTRATION

When you develop registration forms, think about how you ask for attendees' names. What information do you actually need? The form should specify what information you are requesting and how it will be used. If the legal name is not relevant, do not ask for it. If it is, note why. Always put the name of use on the badge itself so people are not forced to out themselves by wearing it.

Include a pronoun field in the registration. If people choose to fill it out, print their pronouns on the badge below the name. This field should be optional and fill-in-the-blank, and there should be a note about how the information will be used. If salutations or honorifics are used on badges, registration confirmations, mailings, or anything else to do with the event, make sure to ask for these instead of assuming them based on name. This field should also be optional and, ideally, fill-in-the-blank. If it must be multiple-choice, include the salutation *Mx.* (usually pronounced "mix"), which is the gender-neutral equivalent of *Mr./Ms.* Some conferences now offer pronoun ribbons that can be attached to badges. This is better than nothing, and it is helpful for anyone who did not supply them at registration but later changes their mind. However, pronoun ribbons (or buttons, or stickers) do not have the same effect as printing pronouns on the badges themselves, as they are quite literally an add-on. They are also not as inclusive unless all attendees fill them out themselves. Often only *he/him*, *she/her*, and *they/them* options are available. It is not reasonable to try to supply all of the possible pronouns, but preprinted options only for some people is othering to those who need to create their own. I, for one, have terrible handwriting and have trouble creating something that looks legible enough to feel professional. It is not a bad idea to supply pronoun ribbons, but this should be in addition to asking pronouns on the registration form. For more details on how to ask people's names and pronouns, see Chapter 3, "Personal Information."

❝━━━   EXAMPLE LANGUAGE
━━━❞

Registration form:

Name of use (for conference badge and communications): _____

_____

Legal name, if different (for billing purposes only): _____

_____

Pronouns (optional; these will appear on the name badge): _____

_____

PRONOUNS

Conferences usually entail many introductions, making them an excellent place to practice pronoun sharing. If you are simply attending as an individual, try to remember to include yours when you meet new people or ask a question at a session. If you are a presenter, include your pronouns on any title slide, bio, or other documentation that accompanies your session. If you are a moderator, encourage people in your session to share their pronouns as they participate. See Chapter 2, "Pronouns and Other Language," for specific guidelines on how to do these things. If you are moderating a panel or introducing a presenter, make sure you know what name and pronouns they

EXAMPLE LANGUAGE

Introducing yourself:

"I'm Stephen. My pronouns are he/him or they/them."

"I'm Stephen; I use he/him or they/them pronouns."

On a presentation slide:

Stephen G. Krueger

Pronouns: he/him or they/them

Access & Outreach Services Librarian

Moderating a group:

"Please introduce yourself with your position and the name and pronouns you'd like us to use for you. If you prefer not to share any of that information, just skip it."

Before introducing a presenter (ask privately ahead of time, not aloud in front of the audience):

"Can you tell me what name and pronouns you would like me to use when I introduce you?"

want you to use before starting. The information that you have been provided by the conference may not be what they prefer to go by, so confirm in person before the session begins. As always, nobody should ever feel forced to share their pronouns. There are plenty of valid reasons for not wanting to do so. The goal of sharing them if you are comfortable is to normalize the practice so everyone can choose to do it or not as they prefer.

DRESS CODES

If your event has a dress code, phrase it so that gender is not a factor. This does not need to change any of the actual attire, but nobody should have to wear or not wear something because of their gender identity. Gendered dress codes ignore the existence of nonbinary people and perpetuate gender stereotypes. Instead of "men wear this and women wear this," simply list the acceptable clothing options and do not worry about who wears what.

ASKING FOR FEEDBACK

If you hear of a problematic situation at an event that you are helping to manage, it is natural to want to find out more so that you can be more inclusive in future. However, be careful how you handle the interaction. It is not the responsibility of any marginalized person to educate you; conversely, it is your responsibility to make the event equally welcoming to everyone, and that may involve research on your part. The same best practices apply here as in any situation where you are trying to educate yourself about an identity that is not your own.

First, reach out to the organization's diversity committee or LGBTQ+ group. If an event occurred in which a trans or gender variant person was treated badly, it is quite possible that this group is already aware. Even if not, they probably will have a good idea of what to do next. If they are willing, let them take the lead on responding. Also provide any support that they ask for; having the most relevant subject knowledge does not mean that it is their responsibility to solve the problem.

Reaching out to the individual(s) affected is not a bad idea, but do it for the right reasons. Let them know that their discomfort matters to the organization and that steps are being taken to avoid any similar situations in future. You can ask if they are willing to share their experience, but do not expect them to do so. It is not the responsibility of any marginalized person to educate the people who mistreated them. Be prepared for anger, and listen rather than defend even if it feels like an attack on something you care about. Explaining away the situation indicates that you are not

 EXAMPLE LANGUAGE

Asking trans and gender variant people about negative experiences:

"I would like to understand more about the situation. Would you be willing to tell me about your experiences or to recommend some resources? Please answer only if you feel comfortable doing so; I know that it is not your responsibility to educate me."

Note: Never ask something like this unless you are fully prepared for a negative response. This language is not a formality; you never have the right to expect anyone to tell you about their experiences. Also do not ask someone based purely on their identity. The place for this question is if there has been a specific event or interaction in which the individual was affected, but do not simply ask a trans person how they feel about something if they are not involved.

actually interested in changing anything, which shows that you do not value the presence of those affected. If you do make changes (and you probably should), let people know that you have done so, but do not assume that they will return. Accept the consequences and try to make more people feel welcome in future.

QUICK FIXES

- Make sure there are all-gender restrooms (with appropriate signage).
- Put name of use and optional pronouns on badges.
- Share pronouns, if comfortable doing so.
- Eliminate gendered dress codes.

LONG-TERM SOLUTIONS

- Be transparent about location decisions.
- Create gender inclusion policy for events.
- Create gender-inclusive restroom policy and share with event staff.

8

Patron Complaints and Employee Objections

Unfortunately, gender inclusion is not yet standardized enough that everyone understands and accepts it, let alone practices it themselves. Sometimes the reason is ignorance (that is, simple lack of awareness that trans and gender variant people exist); sometimes it is bigotry and transphobia. Any of this may occur in a variety of situations. Patrons may complain about materials, employees may object to required trainings, and administrators may resist attempts to make the library more gender inclusive. On the other side, trans and gender variant patrons, employees, and others who strive for gender inclusion may have their own objections and suggestions about how to create an inclusive environment. This chapter offers guidelines and practice scenarios for handling these different situations.

COMPLAINTS FROM PATRONS

Before

It is possible that your library will never have a patron complain about a trans and gender variant issue. However, do not assume that this is out of the question. Of the over 27,000 people who responded to the *2015 U.S. Transgender Survey*, 24 percent had had their presence in a restroom challenged in the previous year (James et al., 2016, p. 226). Two of the top ten most challenged books of 2017, *George* and *I Am Jazz*, made that list for having transgender characters (American Library Association, 2019). Prepare for patron complaints so that you can respond exactly how you want to if they do come up.

Before any complaints actually occur (or before the next one does), take the following steps in whatever form makes the most sense for your library. First, develop clear policies about any library aspect that concerns gender inclusion. Some common topics include collection development, restrooms, and events. These policies should be specific about gender inclusion (see the related chapters for examples). They should be made publicly available on the library website; also consider posting them in the library's physical spaces where relevant. In addition to policies that explain the library's practices, create a system that patrons can use to submit complaints (probably an online and/or print form that will be passed on to the appropriate person or department).

Internally (that is, within the library or particular departments), create a clear process for receiving and responding to patron complaints. The specifics of this depend on the type of complaint and how your library operates. For example, if circulation assistants often work with no supervisor present, they should be trained to respond initially; otherwise, they can simply pass the issue on to a supervisor. A system for handling complaints will allow the library to respond thoughtfully and consistently, rather than forcing an individual employee to react under pressure.

Library policies and the complaint process must be part of employee training. Not everyone has to be intimately familiar with every step, but all employees should know what to do in their position. This is especially important for employees such as part-time circulation assistants, who may not have extensive work experience and should not be expected to respond to patron complaints without specific training in how to do so. Bear in mind that these types of positions are often the first point of contact for patrons, so they may be the ones most often asked to deal with complaints. Whether your system expects them to respond to the patron themselves or to bring in a supervisor, training is essential.

During

1. Listen to the patron and determine what their actual objection is. Take the time to ask questions as necessary, and remember that the situation may not be what you initially assume. If they do not think a book with trans content should be on display, why? They may be transphobic, or they may be concerned because the book contains outdated information that is harmful to trans and gender variant people. If someone comes to the desk with the stereotypical complaint that "there is a man in the ladies' room," find out what they are upset about. Has the patron misgendered someone who is behaving perfectly normally, or is there someone harassing others in the restroom? Trying to address the complaint without enough information is unhelpful and can make the situation worse. Calmly asking the patron to explain will also help them feel heard and respected. If they do have a reasonable concern and are hesitant to bring it up, listening to them will help them feel more comfortable. If they are objecting to something like the presence of trans people in the library, the process of talking it through may help them realize that this is

not a valid complaint. In addition, the conversation will give you some time to determine the best course of action.

 EXAMPLE LANGUAGE

"What is it about this book that bothers you?"

"Are they harassing people or otherwise behaving inappropriately?"

2. Decide whether you can handle the situation on your own. This depends on your position, how your library operates, and how comfortable you feel interacting with the complainant. Perhaps you are a circulation assistant with a supervisor in the next room; in that case, you should probably fetch them and let them handle it. Perhaps you are the supervisor, in which case you may be the most appropriate person to work with the patron. If the complainant seems angry or aggressive, do not hesitate to ask a coworker for support even if they do not have more knowledge than you do. If you are personally involved (e.g., if you are a trans or gender variant library employee and the patron is complaining about your presence in a restroom), definitely find a coworker to help and pull out of the interaction entirely if you need to. If you do not feel equipped to respond to the patron and nobody else is available, such as if you are a circulation assistant working a night shift with no supervisor, provide them with the appropriate person's work phone number or email address and suggest that the patron contact them or return at another time.

 EXAMPLE LANGUAGE

Talking to the patron:

"If you'll wait a moment, I'll get my supervisor; they should be able to help you."

"I can't help you with this question right now, but if you come back during business hours tomorrow someone will be able to. You can also email or leave a phone message and someone will get back to you."

Asking a coworker for support:

"A patron is upset that we have books with trans content on the display. I'm not sure what to do; can you come help?"

"There is a patron who got angry when I used the women's restroom. I'm really uncomfortable; could you please talk to them?"

3. Assuming that you are the correct person to do so, respond to the complaint. If it is a straightforward problem that should be dealt with immediately (such as a person harassing others), obviously take appropriate action. If it is not something that the library should change, such as a book display with no objectionable content, or a person simply using a restroom (remember that you cannot tell a person's gender by how they look, so operate based on the person's behavior instead of trying to determine what restroom you think they should use), show the patron the relevant library policy, explain how it applies to the situation, and volunteer to answer any questions they have. This is why it is so important to have clear and public policies; even if the patron disagrees, they can see that the issue does not violate the library's rules.

 EXAMPLE LANGUAGE

"According to our restroom policy, everyone is encouraged to use the restroom that best suits their gender identity. As long as nobody is harassing people or otherwise behaving inappropriately, we will not ask them to leave."

"We try to make sure that everyone is accurately represented in our library materials. Would you like to see our collection development policy?"

4. Provide the patron with alternative options. This may help redirect their energy in a positive direction, and it reframes the conversation on their responsibility to use the library without interfering with others. Note that you should never ask someone who has done nothing wrong to change their behavior, nor should you remove resources unless they really should not be part of the library's collection. While it may be tempting to find a quick way to make the complainant happy, this is incredibly harmful if they do not have a valid concern. For example, never ask a person to leave a restroom unless their behavior is actually the issue. Instead, suggest alternatives to the person who complained about their presence. If someone objects to a book display on trans topics out of bigotry, offer to help them find other books and ask for suggestions on what displays they would like to see in future. You are under no obligation to take these suggestions, but asking may help the patron feel that you hear and respect them.

EXAMPLE LANGUAGE

"If you are uncomfortable sharing the restroom with someone, you can always wait until they leave. We also have an all-gender restroom that you are welcome to use; that one is single occupancy."

"I'm sorry you don't like this month's display. Can I help you find some books that you will enjoy? If you have ideas for future displays, we always like to get patron suggestions."

5. If the patron remains upset, reiterate library policy. This may not make them happy, but it should be the end of the conversation. You have explained why you will not do what they want, and you have offered them alternatives. This means that the only thing left for them to object to is the fact that the library acknowledges and respects trans and gender variant people. If this is the case, nothing you say will change their mind. If there is a formal complaint system or someone else they should talk to, offer that information, but it is perfectly reasonable to simply repeat the library policy and politely end the conversation.

 EXAMPLE LANGUAGE

"I'm sorry you are upset, but it is against library policy to disrespect anyone by asking them to leave the restroom if they have not behaved inappropriately. You are welcome to use one of the alternatives I mentioned."

"Again, our collection development policy is inclusive of all identities. If you think we should remove a particular title, you can fill out this form and the collection development librarian will review the material to make sure it belongs in the library."

OBJECTIONS FROM EMPLOYEES

Some employees may object when asked to make gender inclusion part of their work. It is important to handle these situations carefully. With some tact and patience, you may be able to make them understand the importance of treating people of all gender identities equitably. You can and should require them to do the same work even if they do not come around on the reasoning behind it, of course, but a hostile work environment is unpleasant for everyone. In *Transgender in the Workplace*, Vanessa Sheridan points out that having expectations for workplace behavior is different from telling employees what to think or believe (Sheridan, 2019, p. 78). This philosophy should be your approach if your employees express reluctance to support trans and gender variant people in the library.

1. As with patron complaints, take the time to listen and try to understand where the employee is coming from. It is possible that they have a concern about how well gender inclusion is being done in your workplace, and you always want people to feel comfortable suggesting improvements. Even if this is not the case, refusing to listen from the start will only create hostility. Ask questions as appropriate, but be careful not to cross any boundaries. Some people claim religion as a reason for disrespecting trans and gender variant people, and you do not want to give anyone an excuse to think that they are being mistreated at work due to their religious beliefs. If it becomes clear that someone's objection is rooted in transphobia or transnegativity, that is the only information you need; you do not need to know where the feeling comes from. It is not likely that you will change their personal thoughts or beliefs, and it is highly inappropriate to attempt to do so.

 EXAMPLE LANGUAGE

"I'm sorry to hear that you didn't find the training helpful. Can you tell me why so that we can avoid issues in the future?"

2. Remind the employee why gender inclusion is an important part of library work and of their job in particular. Try to use a positive approach, and do not suggest that it is optional. Use a clear and matter-of-fact tone that assumes that supporting trans and gender variant people is something that everyone should be doing (because it is). Bring in relevant library policies to support what you are saying.

 EXAMPLE LANGUAGE

"As you know, our nondiscrimination policy includes gender identity and gender expression. This means that we need to take steps to ensure that all of our trans and gender variant patrons and employees feel comfortable here. I know that this may be a new idea to some people, and that is why we have these training sessions."

"It is very important that patrons of all gender identities feel comfortable using the library. This is why you should never tell someone that they can't use a restroom because of what you think their gender is. Let's make a time to review the restroom policy so we're all clear on how staff should be upholding it."

3. End the individual conversation there. The only thing you should be concerned about is that the employee upholds library policy while at work. Do consider whether you can make the workplace expectations clearer in future; if you had trouble finding a library policy that addressed the situation, consider creating one. If the employee's objection came from ignorance rather than bigotry, perhaps more comprehensive job instructions and/or training would help.

CONCLUSION

When faced with a complaint about a trans or gender variant issue, remember what your priorities are. First ensure that any trans or gender variant people involved feel safe. If they have done nothing wrong, give them the option to remove themselves from the interaction entirely, as it is not their responsibility to find a solution to somebody else's ignorance or bigotry. This goes for trans and gender variant library employees, including yourself if you are one—do not be afraid to withdraw from a situation and request that another employee deal with it if you feel uncomfortable. Then work with the complainant to find a solution that fits library policy and feels right to you. Ideally, they will be satisfied also, but this may not be possible if the source of their objection is their own bigotry. For patrons, the best solution may be to let them know library policy, provide alternative options for them, and let them file a complaint. For employees, clearly explain the reasoning behind a practice, but be aware that you may need to simply tell them that inclusive behavior is part of their job and leave it at that. While it is generally your responsibility to try to keep patrons and employees happy in the library, this does not always extend to those whose happiness depends on the oppression or erasure of trans and gender variant people.

QUICK FIXES

- Review library policies, add explicitly gender-inclusive language if it is not already present, and publicly post them (library website and/or relevant physical spaces).
- Develop process for handling complaints.

LONG-TERM SOLUTIONS

- Incorporate patron and employee feedback into future policies and training.
- Train all library employees in how to respond to patron complaints.

REFERENCES

American Library Association. "Top 10 Most Challenged Books of 2017." American Library Association, accessed March 5, 2019, http://www.ala.org/advocacy/bbooks/NLW-Top10.

James, Sandy E., Jody L. Herman, Susan Rankin, Mara Keisling, Lisa Mottet, and Ma'ayan Anafi. *The Report of the 2015 U.S. Transgender Survey*. Washington, DC: National Center for Transgender Equality, 2016.

Sheridan, Vanessa. *Transgender in the Workplace: The Complete Guide to the New Authenticity for Employers and Gender-Diverse Professionals*. Santa Barbara, CA: Praeger, 2019.

9

Library Schools

The faculty and staff of library science programs are uniquely situated to affect how trans and gender variant people experience libraries in the future. Most library workers do not attend library school, but most librarians and many library leaders do. Incorporating gender-inclusive practices into a standard library science education would be an excellent step toward spreading them throughout the profession. Trans and gender variant people are not just potential patrons; we are also present as library students, faculty, and staff. It is therefore the responsibility of all community members to create inclusive environments within library schools as well as outside them.

PERSONAL INFORMATION

The first step in welcoming trans and gender variant people to a library school starts well before their first class. The program's website should have a public nondiscrimination statement for students and employees that explicitly includes gender identity and expression. Faculty and staff bios should include pronouns for those who feel comfortable sharing them. This is an easy way to indicate that the program values gender inclusion; it also normalizes pronoun sharing and may help avoid misgendering of employees.

For student applications, follow essentially the same guidelines as for employees: specify exactly what name and gender information is required and how it will be used, and always refer to applicants by their name of use if it differs from their legal one. See Chapter 5, "Job Postings and Interviews," for specifics on inclusive application language. Once someone has been accepted, make sure that their name of use is what shows on all school paperwork unless the legal name is absolutely necessary. If the library school is limited by the policies of the institution that it is part of, suggest changes to these policies. Put the name of use on class rosters, the online learning

> **❝━ ━❞ EXAMPLE LANGUAGE**
>
> Name of use: _____
>
> Legal name: _____
>
> *Your name of use will show on the school email, learning system, and class rosters. Your legal name will appear on your diploma, campus ID card, and paychecks.*

system, and the school email address so that the student is not outed to professors and classmates. Inform students about what name is used where so that they know what to expect.

Some students transition during their time in the program, so provide clear instructions for how to change the name of use in the school system. Also make sure that all such changes trickle down to class rosters and other documentation. If the legal name must still appear in some places, such as the diploma and student ID, let the student know. This information can be posted on the name change form itself.

GENDER-INCLUSIVE CLASSROOMS

Like all teachers, library science professors are responsible for creating an environment where all students feel comfortable being and expressing themselves. This starts on the first day (or before) with how you learn students' names and pronouns, then continues throughout every course with overt discussions or implied assumptions about gender identity. As trans and gender variant people cannot always assume that people will treat them respectfully, it is the responsibility of the professor to demonstrate that people of all gender identities are welcome in their class.

Nondiscrimination Statements

As with job postings, a full nondiscrimination statement that explicitly includes gender identity and gender expression lets students know that they will not be treated badly because of how they identify or present. Consider including such a statement in your syllabus, whether you adapt language from institutional policy or craft it yourself. The absence of one does not indicate that you will not treat trans and gender variant students inequitably, but stating it clearly removes any question. Also list the contact information for the campus LGBTQ+ center or other support options.

Names and Pronouns

Personal Experience

Before I changed my legal name, I dreaded the first day of classes. Attendance almost always meant that someone would say it in front of the group and I would be forced to respond. Occasionally, a professor would then ask if we wanted to be called something else, but I had already been outed. My program was small enough that I was already out by necessity, as I had transitioned during my time there, but I still hated having to bring it up with every new course. Almost every first class started with discomfort or, if I did not know the professor, fear. I was fortunate enough not to encounter any overt transphobia, but it often took some explanation to get a new professor to use the correct name and pronouns for me. I became accustomed to emailing professors before the first day of class to let them know my correct name and pronouns, which for the most part preempted misgendering.

By contrast, I clearly remember the few professors who took steps on their own. A few asked for pronouns as well as names of use when they first took attendance. One emailed all of her students at the beginning of the semester. Among other things, she asked what name and pronouns we wanted her to use. This approach made me immediately comfortable, as I did not have to dread that first roll call. I also felt acknowledged as a trans person; I did not have to single myself out and take on emotional stress in order to be treated with respect.

The act of taking attendance, depending on how it is done, can cause enormous stress for some trans and gender variant students. Forcing someone to respond to a legal name that they do not use is disrespectful; it can also out them to everyone in the room (as mentioned elsewhere, this is somewhere between rude and dangerous depending on the situation). Even if then you ask for the name of use, you have still publicly identified them using the legal one. The best solution that I have seen came from one of my professors in library school. Before the first day of class, email all of your students and ask what name and pronouns they would like you to use for them (as well as anything else you need to know before classes start). Note any responses on the attendance list so that you remember to use them. This may cause a little extra work for you, but it makes a huge difference to any trans and gender variant people for whom hearing their legal name is painful.

If you choose to have students introduce themselves to each other, invite them to share their pronouns. If you are comfortable doing so, it helps if

EXAMPLE LANGUAGE

"Please respond to this email to let me know what name and pronouns you would like me to use for you in class."

you demonstrate by doing the same. Doing this creates an opportunity for students to let each other know how to refer to them, which helps avoid misgendering. Do not require students to share their pronouns, however, as there are a variety of reasons that some may not wish to do so in a group. It is very important that, having asked, you do whatever is necessary to remember the correct name and pronouns, though mistakes do happen. See Chapter 2, "Pronouns and Other Language," for what to do if you accidentally misgender someone.

For online classes, the process may be a little different depending on how the course is set up. If you are teaching online, familiarize yourself with how participants' names show. Are they automatically drawn from the registrar? If so, are they legal names or names of use? Can students self-identify? It may take a little time to find all this out, so prepare beforehand and contact whoever you need to in order to find out how the system works. If your course management system uses students' legal names, ask if there is a way to change that so students are not forced to use a name they may not feel comfortable with. If participants can choose what name their teacher and classmates see (which is ideal), make sure that everyone is aware of how to do that by emailing them before the course begins. If you do an icebreaker/introduction post, share your pronouns (if you are comfortable doing so) and invite students to do the same.

You may feel that you know all of your students, especially in a small program. In upper-level classes, you may have already met everyone in the room. Regardless, repeat the steps above to learn students' names and pronouns for every new course. If you have a student who has transitioned or changed how they want to be addressed since the last time you taught

 EXAMPLE LANGUAGE

"Tell us what name and pronouns you would like us to use for you, your class year, and your favorite book. If you would prefer not to share any of that information with the group, just leave it out. I'll start: I'm Stephen; my pronouns are he/him or they/them. I am not a student and my favorite book today is *Pansy*, by Andrea Gibson."

> **❝—❞ EXAMPLE LANGUAGE**
>
> "In your first post, introduce yourself. Let us know what name and pronouns you would like us to use for you, what you are hoping to gain from this course, and anything else you feel like telling us. If you would prefer not to share any of this information, leave it out."

them, this saves them the stress of seeking you out to update you individually. Even if their transition seems obvious, never assume that someone feels comfortable talking about it. No student should have to out themselves in order to avoid being misgendered.

Inclusive Language and Examples

Using the correct pronouns for students is not enough. One of the subtler ways in which a professor can create a transnegative classroom environment is by implicitly assuming that the male/female binary applies to everyone. This assumption manifests in a variety of ways. You may not even realize that you are doing it, as the gender binary is deeply ingrained into many societies. First, assess your own perspective and knowledge; you do not need to become a gender theory expert, but you should at least be aware of the existence of people who do not fit into the gender binary. Whether or not you have students who are nonbinary, genderfluid, or something else that is not wholly male or female, avoid perpetuating the gender binary through your language and behavior. For one thing, it can make some people feel invisible or unwelcome, as binary language does not acknowledge their existence. For another, it sets a poor example for library students who will probably end up working with patrons and coworkers of all gender identities.

 Personal Experience

One of my professors used gender for every example of binary opposites. This made me uncomfortable enough that I eventually tried to speak with him about it, but my request that he use literally any other example was met with complete incomprehension. There was simply a total lack of awareness that the gender binary did not apply to everyone. As a first-semester student struggling with my own gender identity, I was not comfortable trying to explain the whole concept to an authority figure, so I just avoided his classes for the rest of the program.

Eliminate binary language whenever you do not explicitly know the gender identity of everyone affected. Do not group students by gender or ask them to self-assign to gendered groups. Avoid referring to people in gendered ways. Instead of "the women" or "the guy in the third row," use neutral phrasing such as "Group A," "the front row," or "the person with the baseball cap."

When providing verbal, written, and visual examples, include nonbinary as well as male and female people. This can be done in lectures, slides, and assignments, both online and in person. For example, a reference class could include an example scenario where a patron is described with *they/them* pronouns. You can use the opportunity to discuss the importance of inclusive language, but the main goal is to normalize nonbinary pronouns so that students know how to work with people who use them.

While real-life examples are important, do not expect trans and gender variant people to share their personal experiences. We are also not automatically experts on everything to do with gender. If you find yourself or your students turning to the one openly trans person in the room when discussing gender, take steps to counter that habit. Think-pair-share is a good tool for this, as it ensures that everyone participates and removes some of the pressure to say the right thing in front of the group. Also use whatever other techniques you usually use when students are reluctant to participate.

PROFESSIONAL DEVELOPMENT

Whether it takes the form of academic coursework, individual sessions, or something else entirely, library schools often offer training in professional skills such as writing cover letters or interviewing. Whoever leads such training should follow the same best practices as anyone else regarding how they learn students' names and pronouns, but that should go without saying at this point. There are several more specific ways in which gender inclusion comes up in this context.

When teaching students about professional expectations, make all guidelines gender neutral. Dress is the most obvious example of this. Instead of telling students that women should wear one thing to an interview and men another, offer a list of acceptable outfit alternatives and leave the choice up to the individual. This helps not only trans and gender variant students. Gendered dress codes perpetuate outdated stereotypes that harm cisgender people as well. Female people should not be pressured to wear dresses and makeup, any more than male people should be shamed for doing the same. If there are other unnecessarily gendered guidelines in your training, reassess them as well. However, also prepare students for the possibility of ending up in environments that enforce oppressive gender norms. Do not tell anyone what to do in such a situation, but do let students know that they may come across individuals and institutions with outdated and prejudiced views. It is important to acknowledge that, while something like a gendered dress code may be an inconvenience for some, it actively denies the gender identities of others, especially nonbinary people. Nobody should be told to present in a way that does not match their gender identity, but some trans and gender variant people find themselves forced to decide between complying and losing a valuable professional opportunity. When training library students for professional scenarios, provide support (practical resources as well as personal sympathy) for those struggling with the realities of a prejudiced work environment.

Normalize gender-inclusive practices. It is up to individual students whether they choose to share their pronouns, but everyone should know how to do so in a professional setting. Demonstrate through examples and verbal practice, and be prepared to answer questions if students are unclear on the purpose. Email signatures, CV and cover letter headers, business cards, and verbal introductions are all places where students should consider sharing their pronouns. See Chapter 2, "Pronouns and Other Language," for more information.

Educate students on name expectations. Trans and gender variant people, as well as anyone else whose name of use differs from their legal one, often hesitate over what name to put on job applications and other professional documents. Using one's legal name is often extremely painful; it can also out someone or cause confusion during the interview process. However, people may fear that putting their name of use will cause the application to be rejected because it does not match their legal documentation. To my knowledge, putting one's name of use on application materials is fine as long as one shares the legal one in the case of a background check. In group sessions and written guidelines, let students know the legal requirements and expectations for names on applications. Also offer to work with students individually, as there are a great many variables (legal name changes, name and pronouns used by references, old transcripts, etc.) that they may need help working through. For example, talk to them about how to contact the HR office of a potential employer to clarify regarding their legal name and name of use. It may be helpful to practice or talk through scenarios like asking an old employer to use one's new name and pronouns. Be prepared to provide emotional support, as the subject of one's legal or previously legal name is very difficult for many trans and gender variant people to talk about. They may not be sure how to raise the subject with you, and they may also simply be worried about how potential employers will react. Affirmation and concrete information are both good ways of supporting people in this situation.

CURRICULUM AND COURSE CONTENT

Some library schools offer a "diversity course" (I took one called Information Services in a Diverse Society). This is certainly better than nothing, but unless it is a required part of the core curriculum, most students will not end up taking it. This is not an effective way of standardizing gender-inclusive practices in library work, as people self-select who learns them. Those who most need training in the subject are those least likely to study it, while LGBTQ+ students will do more of the work that is already implicitly assigned to them. Diversity courses are, by definition, overviews; they may attempt to cover race, gender, sexual orientation, disability, class, and other topics all in one semester, which makes in-depth study of any one area impossible. I would like to see this type of course required for all library students so that everyone gets at least that broad overview.

I think that the most effective way of incorporating gender-inclusive practices into a library education is to integrate them into every subject. One of the major points of this book is that these practices should be part of all aspects of library work, not added on when time and staffing allow. Subject experts are the ones best qualified to determine specific best practices, provided they have educated themselves on trans and gender variant identities enough to do the work respectfully (which they should be doing). Individual professors may not be sure where to start, and changing course content takes time and labor. Therefore, library schools should provide their faculty with Safe Zone and gender inclusion training as well as the resources to spend time updating their courses.

There is no subject in which gender inclusion is irrelevant. Public services are the most obvious, but I can think of no library position that does not have a human interaction component. Few people have no coworkers at all, and most library positions involve patron or subject information even if they do not work with people face-to-face. All library work deals with language and information, both of which have subtle and overt ways of perpetuating gendered societal norms. This shows in collection development and classification as much as in public services. If you are unsure how gender inclusion ties into your discipline, start by researching it as you would any new topic; you will probably find more than you expect. If this fails, reach out to other faculty, campus library workers, or external groups (such as subject-specific listservs or ALA's Gay, Lesbian, Bisexual, and Transgender Round Table) to see if others have explored the topic. If not, it is probably past time that someone do so.

I am not a library professor, and I am not going to attempt to tell anyone how they should teach a subject that I am no expert in. Trans and gender variant issues may not come readily to mind for those with no personal experience in them, however, so I will suggest a few ways in which they can be incorporated into a library education. These are by no means the only ones,

Community Voices

When we talk about equity and inclusion in library school, it is often from the perspective of librarians as a privileged population providing services to marginalized populations. This includes the rare occasions when we talk about providing services to transgender patrons. There's almost never discussion of what to do when we, the library staff, belong to a marginalized population. At the New England Library Association conference in October 2018, I attended a panel on Queering the Library that made many good and explicit suggestions about providing better services to patrons and making the workplace more inclusive to staff. That kind of cohesiveness is largely absent from the LIS curriculum that I have been exposed to in my time in library school.

—Puck Malamud, ve/ver/vis/verself, graduate student

but they may serve to demonstrate how all subjects should include some component of gender inclusion.

- Catologing: Provide instruction and examples on cataloging trans authors (for example, whether to put the legal name in the author record of someone who does not use it, or how to handle the record of an author who publishes under one name, transitions, and then publishes under another). Also discuss how to accurately and respectfully classify and organize works about trans subjects, including awareness about some of the ways in which Library of Congress and Dewey Decimal systems perpetuate the oppression of marginalized populations. See Chapter 12, "Collection Development," for some resources on cataloging.

- Research methods: Teach how to respectfully collect information about names and gender. My teacher actually did this, which was amazing; we spent a class period looking at different ways that surveys asked about gender and assessing their pros and cons.

- Reference: Include practice scenarios with trans or gender variant patrons and topics. Discuss how to choose respectful search terms, given that some older material in this area uses outdated language that some people now find offensive. Also talk to students about what to do when a patron wants help with a problematic question, such as information on trans people harassing others in restrooms (which is a wholly incorrect but dismayingly widespread idea).

- Public services: Train students to interact with patrons without assuming gender identity (for example, eliminate gendered language and list all restroom options if asked). Also prepare students to respond to situations like those outlined in Chapter 8, "Patron Complaints and Employee Objections."

- Metadata/databases/systems: Address how patron and employee names are collected and seen by library workers. Normalize names of use as the default for checkout screens and other places to avoid outing people.

- Instruction: Teach how to respectfully learn pronouns and names of use in long-term and one-shot library classes.

- Management: Discuss how managers can create gender-inclusive workplaces and emphasize the importance of actively doing so. Include trans and gender variant topics (such as adding all-gender restrooms to a library, or dealing with an employee who consistently misgenders coworkers) in case studies, scenarios, and assignments.

- Collection development: Train students to assess the currency and reliability of resources about trans and gender variant subjects. Explain the importance of frequent updating and weeding, as information and current language about gender change over time.

TRAINING

I am a firm believer that anyone who works with other people, even indirectly, should go through training on LGBTQ+ identities. The most common version of this is Safe Zone, which is offered on campus by many colleges and universities. All faculty and staff of library schools should be required to participate in this training. If you have an LGBTQ+ Center or equivalent, contact them to learn the best way to get it. They may be willing to run a session specifically for your program's employees. Participants often get a sign to post on their office door that indicates that they have gone through the training and are a safe person with whom to talk about LGBTQ+ issues. Requiring employees to undergo it does provide everyone with some basic knowledge, but it also means that not everyone who does it is an ally or a safe resource for LGBTQ+ students. Therefore, make the sign optional; everyone should do the training, but they can then choose whether they want to post it on their door. Employees can also note in their website bios or on their course syllabi that they are Safe Zone trained, but this should also be optional. Safe Zone training should be repeated every few years so that employees have current information. Also consider requiring Safe Zone training for all students so that all graduates have gone through it. This is a good way to ensure that they are entering the profession with at least some knowledge about LGBTQ+ people and how to interact with them respectfully, and it will give graduating students an extra line on their CV.

QUICK FIXES

- Include optional pronouns on employee bios on program website.
- Put students' names of use on emails, course rosters, and the course management system.

- Add pronouns and gender inclusion statement to syllabi.
- Email students before each course to learn pronouns and names of use.
- Eliminate gendered language and add gender-inclusive examples in class.
- Use gender-neutral professional guidelines.

LONG-TERM SOLUTIONS

- Require regular Safe Zone training or equivalent for all faculty, staff, and students.
- Incorporate gender inclusion into existing subjects.
- Add course content on gender inclusion to the core curriculum.
- Work with the institution to create more inclusive practices (such as name of use on student ID).

10

Academic Libraries

For the most part, the information in the rest of this book applies to college and university settings as much as it does anywhere else. There are, however, some situations that primarily arise in those environments. This chapter is about the particular experiences of trans and gender variant people in academic libraries. I freely admit that academic libraries are no more important or unique than any other type of library, but this is the field in which I have the most experience, so here we are. There is not much of an order to the content, as there are a variety of different ways in which academic library

 Community Voices

By setting an example of trans inclusivity within our own services, spaces, and systems, libraries are positioned to positively impact the experience of trans, non-binary, and gender non-conforming people campus-wide. We provide an unusual microcosm in which these folks interact with employees who may or may not respect or understand their identities, encounter resources that could or could not represent them, and use spaces that do or do not welcome them. It is possible to weave inclusion throughout a trans individual's library experience, but it's not enough to focus only on our own organizations. Using the expertise we develop and the trans-affirming practices we embody, library workers can and should advocate beyond our own walls for better treatment of trans, non-binary, and gender non-conforming people across institutions of higher education.

—Char Booth, Associate Dean of the University Library at California State University San Marcos, they/them/theirs

workers can support trans and gender variant students and other campus community members.

TRANS AND GENDER VARIANT STUDENTS

Trans and gender variant college students may have similar experiences as other trans and gender variant people, but there are some that are specific to the age and lifestyle of conventional students (that is, 18–22-year-olds who are living away from home for the first time but still rely on parental support). If you work with many patrons who fit this description, consider the following factors as well as the general information in the rest of the book.

For many students, college is the first place where they are able to safely explore their own gender identity. Sometimes this is due to lack of representation in their previous context; meeting openly trans and gender variant people for the first time may be what helps someone figure out their own gender. Some students may have been fully aware of their gender identity but come from a trans-hostile environment where they were unable to safely express it; they may take time to realize that they can safely express their true gender. If a student comes out to you, ask if they want that information widely known or if you should keep it to yourself. This is especially important if you are likely to meet their parents; outing a person to transphobic family members is extremely harmful.

As always, you cannot tell someone's gender by looking at them. In the case of college students, some may not be able to present exactly as they want to. Those who do plan to physically transition may not be able to without outing themselves to their parents; even if they are out, families may be unwilling or financially unable to pay the cost of transition. Other students may not want to physically transition at all, or they may not be ready to do so for any number of reasons. Nonbinary people present in all sorts of ways (as do cisgender and binary trans people, for that matter). None of this makes anyone's gender identity less valid.

Trans and gender variant college students are often navigating an unfamiliar system that enforces gender in unique ways. Gendered dorms and misgendering by professors are a few examples; others vary by institution based on how inclusive the practices are. Be aware that your students may be experiencing all sorts of stressful and traumatic situations, and consider providing emotional support as well as a library environment where they can feel comfortable.

Given all of the difficulties trans and gender variant students face, it is extremely important that the campus library respect them and provide an environment where they can feel safe. Failure to do this is a failure to adequately support the students. If you need a more mercenary reason, consider that it will simply make them stop using the library. Library employees can help by creating an explicitly supportive environment so students know they can safely be themselves. Sharing pronouns, providing all-gender restrooms, and recommendations found elsewhere in this book will help do that. It is the responsibility of all academic library employees to support trans and gender variant students in all possible ways.

PATRON NAMES

Unlike some types of libraries, many academic libraries do not have control over the name on a patron's account; borrower data is usually uploaded from a centralized accounting system, so there is no library card application. This means that you as a librarian cannot decide whether and how to ask for legal name and name of use when a patron applies for a card. However, this does not mean that you cannot adopt inclusive practices for names in patron accounts. How you go about it will vary depending on your ILS, what information the school collects, and who has control over patron accounts, but here are a few elements to consider.

What are the institutional constraints? Some schools allow students to put a name of use on their record. When done properly, this becomes the name that shows on class rosters, email addresses, communications, and all other places that do not absolutely require the legal name. Usually, however, the student ID shows the legal name. Before determining how to handle names in the library, familiarize yourself with campus practices so that you know what limitations or opportunities exist. Do not be afraid to point out issues; if the school has no name of use option for students, contact the registrar and strongly suggest that this be added.

What are your system's constraints? One ILS may operate completely differently from another, so speak with your systems administrators to learn how yours handles patron names. Does it use only legal names, or is there a name of use field? How are data for new student accounts loaded into your ILS (directly from a campus Enterprise Resource Planning system, or manually entered by library employees)? Also learn who has control over the system. Do you have a systems administrator with the power to add a name of use field, or does that have to go through the software vendor? As with institutional constraints, communicate with the company if you want something changed.

How do you handle name changes? Trans and gender variant students (not to mention faculty and staff) may change their legal name or name of use while at the school. How are these changes reflected in the ILS? Does the new information trickle down from the registrar, or can library employees change it manually upon request? If a student changes their name in the institutional system, will that information be passed on to the library, or do they need to tell you separately? Is there a clear way to do this, or do they just have to out themselves to a circulation assistant and hope for the best?

What information do circulation employees see? When a student checks out a book, are they automatically outed by their student ID or the information on the screen? How can this be avoided? If your system has a name of use option, that should be what shows whenever the account is opened. The legal name should never appear. If the campus ID shows the student's legal name, consider creating a separate library card using the ID number as the identifier.

How are your circulation employees trained? Whatever the specifics of your system, develop best practices for interacting with patrons. If the ILS must show legal names, train your circulation employees to avoid saying them aloud. If a student can request that their name be changed in the ILS, make sure all circulation employees know how the process works.

How do you share information with students? You may have a perfect, inclusive system, but this does not mean much if students do not know about it. Do not leave it up to trans and gender variant students to come to the circulation desk if they want their name of use added to the ILS; this is deeply stressful even if one knows it is an option. Use the library website and additional communication methods to share information. Make it clear who will see their name of use; communications sent to a student at home or to their parents can inadvertently out them to family.

Personal Experience

I came out and transitioned during graduate school. During my second year, I was in the process of changing my legal name and starting hormones. Both of these are slow processes, and I was often misgendered by faculty and other students. Like most that I have seen, the campus libraries used our student ID as our library card. The ID and the ILS showed my legal name, which I was deeply uncomfortable using at the time. Because of this, I would decide whether or not to check out a book based on whether I had the emotional energy to deal with misgendering that day (sometimes it was worth it, sometimes not).

An important element of this situation is that I was not a typical library user. I was in my second year of the LIS program; I also worked in that library, and though I did not work at the circulation desk, many of those who did were my friends, classmates, and coworkers. Even so, I was not comfortable checking out a book. If this was true for me, with all of my investment in libraries in general and that library in particular, I can only imagine how undergraduates and other students without that investment must feel. It would be incredibly easy to simply stop using the library rather than face constant misgendering, and I am certain that some people make that choice.

When I did work up the nerve to say something, the response was extremely positive. The head of access services took immediate action, though the constraints of the system meant that "action" was a discussion with the department that controlled the ILS. What really struck me was the realization that there was no malice in the system's cisnormativity; it had simply never occurred to anyone there that someone might not want to use their legal name. That unintentional ignorance, however, meant that the library's practices made some patrons extremely uncomfortable.

You may feel frustrated because you have no control over the systems you use. Do not discount the value of suggesting change to someone else. This may be a library department, the campus registrar, or the company that develops your ILS. Perhaps they simply have never considered the importance of a name of use field and will be happy to add one at your suggestion; perhaps it is on their enhancement list and repeated reminders from library customers will help it happen faster. Either way, it is worth letting the people who can influence change know you want to see a name of use field added. Follow up periodically to check for status updates. Meanwhile, train your employees to work within the constraints of the system to treat trans and gender variant students respectfully.

STUDENT WORKERS

The hiring process for student workers is usually less formal than it is for full-time positions. However, this is no excuse for making it less inclusive. How one goes about this may vary, so review Chapter 5, "Job Postings and Interviews," and see if anything there can be adapted to your library's process. Because college students may not express their gender identities in traditional ways, either by choice or because of the limitations described above, it is the responsibility of supervisors to limit misgendering of our student workers.

This starts before a student's first shift at the library. When communicating privately with students to set up an interview, ask their name and pronouns. I mix this in with several other preliminary questions (class year, hours of availability, etc.) to normalize it. Do not be surprised if they do not answer; some students may simply not understand the question, and others may prefer not to say. The goal is to provide a way for those who want to share their name of use and pronouns to do so easily, not to require that they tell you these things.

 EXAMPLE LANGUAGE

"What name and pronouns would you like me to use for you?"

Like any customer service position, employment at a circulation desk comes with regular misgendering for many trans and gender variant people. Since this is where most student assistants work, take steps to help them avoid misgendering by patrons. Nametags with optional pronouns are one way to do this. Before or during training, ask new student workers what name and, if any, pronouns they would like on their nametag. It is important to make the pronouns optional, as some students may be uncomfortable having theirs displayed (see Chapter 2, "Pronouns and Other Language," for more information on why people might not want to share their pronouns publicly). Depending on the size of the school, student workers may know some or all of their patrons. Nametags with pronouns may assist them with letting classmates and professors know how they would like to be referred to, but they may also not be out to everyone they will interact with at work. Therefore, wearing the nametags should be optional. Be sure to let student workers know you are happy to make a new nametag for them if they change what they want on it.

Personal Experience

In a delightful turn of events, I have access to a button maker. This means that I can easily make nametags for all of my student assistants. When planning the design (which was done by one of the student workers), I asked that the buttons have a space for pronouns that would not look odd if left blank, so that everyone can decide for themselves what information should go on it. The result is a satisfying mixture: some but not all of the trans students want pronouns, as do some but not all of the cisgender students. One nonbinary student was out to library staff but did not want their pronouns on their nametag at first; eventually they decided they were ready to share them and requested a new nametag. Gender identity is not the only relevant factor; students who use a nickname or other name of use, including many international students, usually prefer to have those on their nametags. Some students are unfamiliar with the practice of pronoun sharing, so I show them examples of nametags with and without when asking what they want on theirs. I and some of the other full-time employees have similar ones, which helps normalize the practice.

LIBRARY INSTRUCTION

For long-term courses taught by library employees, best practices are basically the same as for any academic course (see Chapter 9, "Library Schools," for guidelines on those). However, these techniques do not always fit the common one-shot model of library instruction; for example, one usually does not have the same level of communication with students beforehand or enough class time for introductions. This does not mean that gender inclusion is not important for one-shots, just that a different approach is required. Please note that I am not an instruction librarian, so the following ideas may not apply directly to your classes. Adapt them as needed to fit.

Student Interaction

Even if you do not have time for student introductions, you probably start by introducing yourself. Always share your pronouns if you are comfortable doing so. If the session is interactive and you will be talking to individual students, consider providing temporary nametags and suggesting that they put their name of use and pronouns on them. You could provide premade buttons with pronouns on them, though this does leave out anyone whose pronouns are not available (self-identification is always better than prese-lected options). This style of nonverbal name and pronoun sharing gives students space to self-identify and helps you avoid misgendering them. In combination with your own pronoun sharing when you introduce yourself, it lets students know that you are actively trying to create a gender-inclusive space, which may make them feel more comfortable talking to you (in general as well as about trans and gender variant topics). When talking to and about students, use the best practices for gender-inclusive language outlined in Chapter 2, "Pronouns and Other Language." Avoid grouping students by gender identity, and use gender-neutral language when you call on or describe them.

Gender-Inclusive Lesson Ideas

There are a number of ways to include trans and gender variant content in library instruction sessions. As with any lesson plan ideas, these do not need to be included every time, but consider adding them where they make sense. If done well (that is, if you use current language and are respectful of the trans and gender variant people in your examples), this demonstrates to students that you are someone who can be safely asked for research help on other trans and gender variant topics. Remember that this cannot always be assumed, so some students may be hesitant to raise the subject with a stranger.

General instruction is a good place to incorporate trans and gender vari-ant topics. For example, a lesson on assessing news sources could use the transgender military ban (Liptak, 2019) or Christine Hallquist's nomination as the first out transgender major party candidate for governor (Schmidt and Epstein, 2018). These events are relevant at the time of the writing of this book, but you can draw more current ones based on when you are planning the lesson. Also try to highlight material about trans people of color, trans people with disabilities, and nonbinary people. Varied examples demonstrate the range of people who make up the trans and gender variant community. Including trans subject matter in this way helps normalize the existence of trans and gender variant people, who are often erased simply through lack of representation.

There are some lessons where explicitly discussing gender is appropriate. When looking at data, discuss with students how gender identity is represented and what that means as far as who is counted and who gets erased. For example, any survey that asks if respondents are male or female does not count nonbinary people (and, if the gender question is required, forces them to choose a gender identity that is not theirs in order to participate). If you are teaching students about authority as a factor of resource quality, the identity of authors writing on a trans subject is a possible example. Discuss how identity may be a factor but is not a substitute for training and education for scholarly work. Also consider how the identity of the author may be more or less relevant given the genre—if a cisgender person is writing an editorial supporting antitrans legislation, what is their motivation? In fiction, is author identity an important factor in how well a book represents trans and gender variant characters? Do not try to cover this information if you are unsure how to discuss it, but consider how to do so in a classroom or research support setting.

WORKING GROUPS AND CAMPUS RESOURCES

While individuals or departments can do a lot of the work described above and in the rest of this book on their own, it is far better to establish long-term plans and policies for gender inclusion. If possible, establish a working group to assess the current status of your library and make plans for the future. This may have been done or be in progress by your institution already; in that case, ask how the library can participate, but that is no reason not to create a library-specific version also. One resource available to many academic libraries is the campus LGBTQ+ Center (or equivalent). Not all schools have one, but many larger ones do. Some smaller places may have a general multicultural services office or something similar, which may or may not cover LGBTQ+ issues. If your institution has one, reach out for support as you make long-term plans for gender inclusion. You do not need to reinvent the wheel; excellent examples of reports already exist, such as the campus-wide one by the CSUSM Trans & Gender Non-Conforming Task Force (2017) and the library-specific one from Virginia Commonwealth University (White et al., 2018). A good report will have particular plans based on its spaces, resources, and community, but you can find a framework that you like and adapt it to your own needs.

QUICK FIXES

- Find out name of use options on campus and in ILS.
- When teaching, share pronouns with students and provide ways for them to share theirs.
- Provide ways for student assistants to share name of use and pronouns if they want to.

LONG-TERM SOLUTIONS

- Create a gender inclusion working group.
- Change (or ask company to change) ILS to prioritize name of use field.
- Incorporate trans content into library instruction.

REFERENCES

CSUSM Trans & Gender Non-Conforming Task Force. *Report & Recommendations*. San Marcos, CA: California State University San Marcos, 2017. https://infomational.files.wordpress.com/2009/06/csusm-trans-gender-non-conforming-task-force-report-recommendations-2017.pdf.

Liptak, Adam. "Supreme Court Revives Transgender Ban for Military Service." *The New York Times*, January 22, 2019. https://www.nytimes.com/2019/01/22/us/politics/transgender-ban-military-supreme-court.html.

Schmidt, Samantha, and Kayla Epstein. "Christine Hallquist Wins Vermont Primary, Becoming first Openly Transgender Major Party Nominee for Governor." *The Washington Post*, August 15, 2018. https://www.washingtonpost.com/news/morning-mix/wp/2018/08/15/christine-hallquist-wins-vermont-primary-becoming-first-openly-transgender-major-party-nominee-for-governor/.

Smith-Borne, Holling. "Best Practices for Creating a Welcoming Environment for Transgender and Gender Non-Conforming Individuals in Libraries." In *Brick & Click: An Academic Library Conference*, edited by Frank Baudino, Kathy Hart, and Carolyn Johnson, 109–118. Maryville, MO: Northwest Missouri State University, 2017. https://files.eric.ed.gov/fulltext/ED578189.pdf#page=116.

White, Erin, Donna E. Coghill, M. Theresa Doherty, Liam Palmer, and Steve Barkley. *Gender-Inclusive Library Workgroup Report*. Richmond, VA: Virginia Commonwealth University, 2018. https://scholarscompass.vcu.edu/libraries_task/1/.

11

Access Services

Perhaps the most influential factor in whether someone feels comfortable in a library is the experience they have when checking out a book. This includes the verbal and nonverbal interactions with circulation staff, the way interlibrary loan (ILL) and hold items are labeled, what personal information they must provide in order to use the library, and how library employees respond to complaints. As always, the general information found earlier in this book should be applied everywhere, but this chapter is designed to cover situations relevant to access services.

CIRCULATION

Nonverbal Cues

Interpersonal interactions are just one part of how libraries make trans and gender variant patrons feel welcome. An inclusive library atmosphere (including, for example, all-gender restrooms with good signage, and collections and displays that acknowledge trans and gender variant people) indicates that one can safely engage with the staff. Behind-the-scenes elements like restroom policies and staff training are another aspect of gender inclusion. All of these elements complement each other, and none should stand alone. It is very important for the circulation staff to use gender-neutral language, but lack of an all-gender restroom can still make a space unwelcoming to some people. Conversely, trans and gender variant books should be part of the collection, but patrons may not feel comfortable checking them out if circulation staff misgender them during the interaction.

For circulation staff, gender inclusion starts before you even speak to patrons, and nonverbal cues may help a trans or gender variant patron feel comfortable talking to library workers. At the circulation desk, nametags with pronouns are one such cue. If you are in charge of designing and creating nametags for circulation staff and other employees or volunteers, add an optional pronoun field. Leave it up to individuals whether they want pronouns on theirs, but do point out the option so that they know it is available. See Chapter 2, "Pronouns and Other Language," for more information. If you do not have nametags or if they do not have pronouns on them, you can get or create pronoun buttons or stickers. Managers can make these available for employees, but individuals can also get their own and wear them at work. If you are a manager or supervisor, clearly explain the benefits of nonverbal pronoun sharing and other gender-inclusive behavior, especially to employees who regularly interact with patrons. Trans and gender variant people often feel invisible, so we may be more willing to engage with people who have indicated that they acknowledge and respect our existence.

Verbal Interactions

When you speak to or about patrons (or anyone else, for that matter), use gender-inclusive language. Do this with everyone, as you cannot know someone's gender or how they want to be described unless they explicitly tell you. If you do know this information about someone, of course, use whatever language they have asked you to use for them. See Chapter 2, "Pronouns and Other Language," for more detailed information on what to say and why, but here are a few common examples of inclusive language at the circulation desk:

- Neutral language: Avoid gendered terms unless you know the gender identity of the person in question. When you use gendered language, you are deciding which term to use for a person based on how they look, sound, or act. While you may often be correct, it is not worth the risk of misgendering someone. It is not merely a matter of correctly deciding which term to use for a person; gendered language does not acknowledge nonbinary people at all, so the way to avoid misgendering is to use neutral language for everyone.
  - Omit gendered honorifics: (sir/ma'am/Mr./Ms./Miss/Mrs.)
  - Use neutral descriptors ("the patron in the blue shirt" instead of "the woman in line")
  - Use neutral pronouns for individuals (*they/them* instead of *she/her* or *he/him*)
- Names: If your library puts patrons' legal names on their library cards, accounts, or ILL paperwork, do not use these when speaking to a patron. Remember that the name you see may not be the one the patron goes by.
- Restroom directions: When someone asks where the restrooms are, point out all of them instead of whichever one you assume they should be using. This prevents you from misgendering the patron and lets them choose for

themselves. They may also want the information for someone else, so this practice is about more than gender inclusion.

- Share your pronouns: If you are leading an event or otherwise in a position to introduce yourself, share your pronouns if you are comfortable doing so.

Patron Information

For specific guidelines, see Chapter 3, "Personal Information." This section contains some highlights that are relevant to circulation.

Unless your library has a specific reason for doing so, do not require patrons' legal names. The application form should have a name of use field (including an explanatory note in case the term is unfamiliar). If you must, ask for ID and/or proof of address when the patron applies, but do not put the legal name on the account without a concrete reason. If your library does require this, also include a name of use field, along with a note about how the legal name will be used and who will see it. Be aware that disclosing one's legal name is incredibly stressful for some trans and gender variant people because it can force us to out ourselves, often to a stranger who may react with confusion or hostility (even if you trust yourself and/or your employees not to react badly, the patron has no way of knowing this).

---

66 ═══   **EXAMPLE LANGUAGE**
═══ 99

Name of use* _____

Name of use is the name you want on your library account. It does not need to match your legal name.

Hold Shelf

Public hold shelves are problematic for all aspects of patron privacy, but some libraries do have them. Many patrons may feel uncomfortable having their reading choices publicly shown, often in a prominent location near the circulation desk. Trans and gender variant people have the additional concern of other patrons seeing what materials they have requested and making assumptions about their gender. This is especially the case in a small community where patrons may know each other and be able to identify whose hold item is whose. Even if someone is out as trans or gender variant, they should have control over where and how that information is shared (especially with strangers, given the discrimination and violence against trans and gender variant people). If you must have a public hold shelf, use an anonymous system such as putting card numbers on books instead of patron names. Also consider creating a private alternative behind the desk and offer the option when a patron places a hold request. One benefit of a public hold shelf is that, if combined with a self-checkout machine, it makes it possible for someone to request and acquire materials that they are self-conscious about without talking to a library employee. However, it is never acceptable to publicly tie identifiable information such as patron names (even parts of them) with specific materials.

Self-Checkout Machines

No matter what you do, some trans and gender variant people will hesitate to approach the circulation desk. The strategies in this book will help you create a more welcoming environment, but that also means providing alternatives so people are not forced into situations where they feel uncomfortable. Even if you have succeeded in creating a library that comprehensively supports trans and gender variant people, it will take time for new patrons to trust that. Face-to-face interactions with strangers are often some degree of negative for trans and gender variant people because they so frequently involve misgendering, microaggressions, or harassment; even if all of your library employees are trained in inclusive behavior, past experiences may make some people hesitant to approach them. If your ILS uses legal names, circulation desk interactions can be very uncomfortable for some patrons. Others may not want to show anyone what materials they are checking out. It is the responsibility of library workers to minimize these concerns, but you cannot decide who should feel safe and comfortable.

Self-checkout machines resolve all of these issues simultaneously. Patrons can use them if they fear judgment or discrimination based on their appearance or the materials they are checking out. The machines also save patrons from being outed or misgendered if their legal name is in the ILS or on their library card. Self-checkouts are not a substitute for any of the work outlined in this book; do not use one as an excuse to eliminate the issues described here. It is still the responsibility of the library and its employees to treat trans and gender variant patrons equitably. In a library with inclusive practices, patrons will be able to interact with circulation workers without fear of judgment, outing, or misgendering. Even then, however, people new to the library can use the machines while they grow comfortable enough to approach the circulation desk without stress.

Interlibrary Loan

Interlibrary loan (ILL) often uses a different system from the one used for circulation. This means that ILL workers need to establish their own best practices for gender inclusion. Specifics will depend on how your library operates, but the main concern is patron names and how they are shown. Ideally, legal name should not be part of a patron's ILL profile at all. Even if it has to be, name of use should be what appears on the account and in all communications. Since many ILL emails and documents are generated automatically, go through your system and check how patron names show in all instances. It is extremely off-putting to get an automated email with a name that one does not feel comfortable using; having the incorrect name on printed paperwork is worse still, as circulation staff and other people see this. Patrons may be outed by their legal name appearing on an ILL book. They may also have to out themselves by telling the circulation staff their legal name so that the book can be located; this is a horrible situation to put anyone in, and it may make them reluctant to use ILL or the library again.

You may have little or no control over how your ILL system processes patrons' names. If this is the case, contact whoever does (probably the company that developed the system) and suggest changes. Encourage others in your field to do the same. If the system accepts only legal names, see if you can work within those constraints to minimize outing and misgendering patrons. For example, start automated emails with a generic greeting instead of a name, and put the patron's first initial instead of their first name on ILL slips.

POLICIES AND TRAINING

Some circulation workers may bring their own gender inclusion knowledge, but others may bring everything from ignorance to active transphobia. You cannot tell employees what to think or believe, but you can tell them how to behave at work. In the context of access services, this means that you can and should have clear, enforceable guidelines on how to respectfully interact with trans and gender variant patrons. Employees should also be made familiar with how the library systems (ILL, hold notices, borrower accounts) handle patron names so that they can behave accordingly. For example, if your ILS uses legal names only, it is especially important that circulation staff not call patrons by the name that shows up on the screen. If the ILS allows name of use for patron accounts, this is less of an issue, though name changes still occur. Your policy for circulation staff behavior should reflect the specifics of your library.

It is insufficient to merely draft policy. Employees must be given enough training to be familiar with both the expectations of the position and the reasoning behind those expectations. If a circulation assistant does not think they have ever met a trans or gender variant person, they may need some background information about what misgendering is and why they should avoid doing it to patrons and coworkers. Simply directing them to avoid gendered language does not convey that information. Inclusive habits are

EXAMPLE LANGUAGE

The library strives to welcome patrons and employees of all gender identities. With this in mind, use the guidelines below to create an inclusive environment. If you have any questions about why you should do these things, or if you have suggestions for making the library more gender inclusive, please talk to [*supervisor/HR/whoever has information about this*].

- Avoid making assumptions about a person's gender. If someone asks where the restroom is, tell them all of the options instead of assuming that they should be using the men's or women's room. Do not call patrons by gendered terms such as *sir* or *ma'am* unless you know that is what they prefer to be called. Remember that *they* is an appropriate gender-neutral pronoun to use for anyone unless they want to be called something else.

- If you are willing to do so, share your personal pronouns when you introduce yourself. ("I'm Stephen, the Access & Outreach Services Librarian. My pronouns are he/him or they/them.") This will make others feel more comfortable sharing their pronouns if they need or want to. You are also encouraged to use the pronoun buttons, located in the circulation office, whenever you are at work.

- Avoid assigning binary gender to groups. For example, if you need to divide a group of children for an activity, use something like Group A/Group B instead of boys and girls. When addressing a group of people, use neutral language like "folks" or "everyone" instead of "ladies and gentlemen." This avoids excluding people who do not identify as male or female.

- Patrons may not want to be called by their legal name. When you create an account for a new patron, put their name of use on the account, even if this differs from the legal name on their ID. The application form reflects this policy by asking only for name of use; use any identification only to confirm identity when the application is submitted.

much easier to develop if one understands the purpose of them and sees how they affect real people.

In my experience, even well-meaning people sometimes struggle with exactly what to do or say in a real-life situation. Training for circulation employees should include scenarios where they can try out the behaviors that they have been told to use. This sort of practice makes unfamiliar language come more naturally; it also provides opportunity for discussion of how trans and gender variant people may feel if treated in different ways. Safe Zone training or an equivalent should be provided for all library employees, but that is usually fairly generalized. Those who work directly with patrons should receive further training that focuses on trans inclusion in interpersonal interactions. If possible, this should be incorporated into general training for new employees. It can also be done as a group workshop or other session for all staff or everyone in a given department. Standardized trainings ensure that everyone has at least a basic level of knowledge on gender inclusion, though individuals may have more based on their own life experiences.

PATRON COMPLAINTS

As the first point of contact for many patrons, the access services department should be prepared to respond to complaints. Chapter 8, "Patron Complaints and Employee Objections," has guidelines and sample scenarios. The short version consists of the following steps:

1. Create clear policies for library practices (restrooms, collection development, events, etc.) and post them on the library website and/or physical spaces so that patrons have access to them.

2. Train circulation staff and other employees who regularly interact with the public on how to respond to patron complaints. The specifics of this depend on your library. Are circulation assistants often working without a manager? If so, they should be trained to respond, at least initially. If there is always a supervisor around, it may be better to train circulation assistants to refer the patron to them instead. Either way, train circulation staff in what to do beforehand so that they know how to react.

3. Determine the actual issue. If it is something that should be dealt with, such as an inappropriately cataloged book or someone harassing others in the restroom, respond accordingly. If not, move on to step 4.

4. Refer the patron to library documentation (such as a restroom policy stating that everyone is welcome in whatever restroom best suits their gender identity).

5. Offer the complainant alternatives so that they can still use the library without interfering with anyone else (for example, help them find books that they do not object to, or point them to the single-occupancy restroom so that they do not have to worry about sharing it).

6. If they persist, determine the best course of action based on the subject and your position. Tell them how to lodge a formal complaint about a book in the collection, ask your supervisor to take over, or simply refer back to the library policy and end the conversation there. It is possible that nothing you say will satisfy the patron; some people will object to any acceptance of trans and gender variant people in public spaces, and you probably cannot change their minds.

QUICK FIXES

- Add optional pronoun fields to nametags of everyone who interacts with patrons.
- Develop a hold shelf system that does not connect titles to patron names.
- Develop circulation and ILL practices that do not use patrons' legal names.
- Provide circulation staff with guidelines and sample language for gender-inclusive behavior.
- Post gender inclusion policies in the library's physical spaces and/or on the website.

LONG-TERM SOLUTIONS

- Provide Safe Zone and gender inclusion training for all access services employees.
- Develop a process for handling complaints and teach it to all employees who work with the public.
- Add a self-checkout machine to the library.

12

Collection Development

WHY HAVE A TRANS-INCLUSIVE COLLECTION?

I hope that I do not need to explain to library workers how important representation is in library collections. For some trans and gender variant people, books (fiction or not) may be one of the few places where we see people like us. Reading may be how we recognize our own identities for the first time, or how we learn that others of that identity exist. In isolated or hostile environments, library books may be the only way for someone to learn information about gender identity and transition. Representation is important for everyone, not just trans and gender variant people. Family and friends of trans and gender variant people may need information about how to support them. A diverse collection normalizes identities that patrons may not be familiar with. Good representation helps make the world safer for trans and gender variant people in all sorts of ways.

Personal Experience

As a child and teenager, I learned about the world primarily through books. The libraries that I frequented had few resources on LGBTQ+ topics, let alone anything trans-specific. I think I was sixteen when I first read a trans character in fiction (Chris Bohjalian's *Trans-Sister Radio*); while I found her sympathetic, she was not the protagonist. It did not occur to me, a teenage girl only barely becoming aware that I might not be straight, to relate to the middle-aged trans woman in the book. The same was true when I saw the movie *Transamerica* not long after. In college I saw *Boys Don't Cry*, which finally had a character similar to what I would later realize was my own identity (albeit one who was brutally murdered at the end).

I do not really blame the libraries and bookstores; the glorious increase in LGBTQ+ representation in YA novels did not take hold until after I graduated college. Still, the lack of trans content in my reading meant that it took me years to realize my own gender and still longer to learn about nonbinary identities. Even now, published works tell palatable, marketable stories. The people I relate to most, fictional and real, come from fanfiction and blog posts.

COLLECTION DEVELOPMENT POLICIES

Collection development policies are relevant to trans content in the same way they are for all other library materials: they help library workers build a coherent and relevant collection. They guide what to purchase and what to weed so that these decisions are not made arbitrarily. For trans and gender variant subject matter, having outdated or inaccurate content can be harmful as well as a waste of shelf space; an active collection development process helps prevent this. When you work to make your library's collection more inclusive, the first step in the process should be a review and update of the collection development policy. Exactly how you do this depends on how your library operates. Include a statement on the value of a diverse collection along with guidelines on how to apply it when selecting materials. Also have a section on weeding criteria. This may be sufficient, or you may want to be more specific. Perhaps you want to include a schedule for assessing the currency and relevance of the collection to ensure that the materials stay up-to-date; this should include weeding as well as addition of new materials. Design your policy based on who will be applying it and how much direction they will need. Also consider how it can be used to support selection or weeding decisions if there are patron complaints.

The collection development policy, or at least a version of it, should be made publicly available on the library's website. This transparency is one way to help trans and gender variant patrons feel more comfortable in the library, though it is probably not likely that many patrons will read it. The more concrete purpose in posting the policy is that you can point to it if patrons object to particular materials. In 2017, books with transgender characters made up 20 percent of the top ten most challenged books (American Library Association, n.d.). Chapter 8, "Patron Complaints and Employee Objections," has guidelines for responding; one recommendation is to create and make public a collection development policy that explains the importance of a diverse collection.

ASSESSMENT FACTORS

When you choose books on trans and gender variant subjects, apply the standards used for all library materials. That said, there are some factors that are especially important or that should be considered in specific ways. I am not a collection development librarian; while I will suggest some things to keep in mind, it is up to you how to apply them in your work.

Currency

The way people think and talk about gender changes all the time, and this is reflected in published material. In some genres, professional guidelines affect how gender identity is described. Medicine and health is the most obvious. The World Health Organization classified being transgender as a mental illness until 2018 (Simon, 2018); the American Psychological Association dropped the term "gender identity disorder," which categorized trans people as having a mental disorder, in 2012 (Lee, 2012). Obviously, it is harmful to find one's gender identity described as an illness or disorder; this outdated language also encourages transphobia and transnegativity. Therefore, libraries should carry updated material that does not use the obsolete terminology. Medical options for trans and gender variant people are improving all the time, so current literature is about up-to-date information as well as language. Nonfiction books about gender identity often cover social and legal issues; these, too, are changing rapidly, so current information is important.

Authority

Does an author have to be trans or gender variant in order for a book or article on those identities to be valuable? No, of course not. For one thing, that would force such authors to out ourselves in order to be taken seriously. For another, no group should be expected to do all of the labor of researching and publishing about themselves; that is logic that assigns people of color to diversity committees regardless of their interest in the subject, and it is terribly harmful. Cisgender people are allowed to write about whatever they like, and so should trans and gender variant people. Unless the gender identity of the author is part of the material, as in the memoir of a trans person who chooses to write about their gender, it has no bearing on the value of the work. When you are assessing a collection as a whole, then you might consider how well authors of various gender identities are represented (see below).

When considering the authority of a resource on trans and gender variant topics, apply the same guidelines as with any other. Look at the author's qualifications, training, and work experience if those are relevant. Also check the publisher, as it is not unusual for antitrans organizations to publish harmful books on gender identity that attempt to pass as legitimate resources. If you cannot learn enough or notice potential issues, look more closely at the contents and reviews.

Representation

This section is less about assessing an individual book and more about seeing how it fits into your collection. The experiences of trans people vary widely even within a single identity, and this is even more the case when race, ability, socioeconomic status, and other elements are considered. When you assess the representation of trans subjects, characters, and authors in your library, acknowledge that variety. A cisgender author may write a perfectly excellent novel with a trans protagonist. However, you have a problem if all of your trans and gender variant characters are created by cisgender writers, or if all of your trans memoirs are by and about white, abled trans men. If you notice a pattern like this, seek out materials in the underrepresented groups and add them to the collection.

Reviews

If you do not have much knowledge about trans and gender variant identities, it may be difficult to tell at a glance whether a book represents them positively. There are a great many transphobic and transnegative books masquerading as reliable literature; sometimes these end up on best-seller lists (Avery, 2018). Look at your usual sources for reviews, such as *Library Journal* or *Choice* if you have access. In addition, seek reviews from an alternate source to get an idea of how trans and gender variant people (or at least advocates sympathetic to us) feel about a book. Perhaps this is an explicitly trans-friendly periodical or website; perhaps it is the comments section of Goodreads. These resources probably should not be your sole reason for purchasing or rejecting a book; however, they may let you know about any red flags regarding the content. Any single reviewer, casual or professional, can be transphobic or just ignorant of relevant information, and a second review from a different perspective may point out something the first missed. The Gay, Lesbian, Bisexual, and Transgender Round Table of the American Library Association releases annual book lists (*Rainbow Book List* for children and teens, *Over the Rainbow* for adults) as well as the annual Stonewall Book Awards and ongoing book reviews. These often include trans content, though they are for all LGBTQ+ material and not trans-specific.

Relevance

It is entirely possible that your library has exceptions to these guidelines. Perhaps you are a special library that collects resources on medical history; perhaps your university's gender studies program regularly assigns projects on historical writings about trans people. As with the rest of this book, this section is designed to be adapted to suit your needs, not used precisely as written. My advice regarding relevance is to put yourself in a standard patron's shoes. Will someone browse the shelves assuming that the information there is current and reliable? In most libraries, this is probably the case. If you do not have a specific reason to have outdated, inaccurate, or otherwise harmful information, do not do so.

WEEDING

In some subjects, weeding may be something to be done as time allows, which often means rarely or never. For books on trans and gender variant topics, leaving outdated information on the shelves can be incredibly harmful. If someone of any identity browses or intentionally looks for information on gender identity, they should be able to trust that the resources provided by the library are current and accurate. Patrons may be reluctant to ask for a librarian's help due to fear of outing themselves or because they are unsure how to talk about the subject; they will see only what is on the shelf. As usual, general weeding standards can be applied. For example, there is no harm in keeping older memoirs of trans and gender variant people, but books on medical transition should be kept as current as possible (which means removing outdated ones as well as acquiring new ones). Write frequent review and weeding into your collection development policy and abide by it.

DISPLAYS AND RECOMMENDATIONS

Displays and recommendation lists let a library showcase particular materials; they can also implicitly demonstrate awareness about a topic or event, indicating to patrons that the library is a supportive space for that subject. After you have created a collection development plan and purchased up-to-date books on trans and gender variant topics, promote them so that patrons know they are available. There are two ways to incorporate these resources into your displays and lists. The first is to create some on trans-specific themes. These can be based around a specific event or topic. Review the Representation section above and apply that approach here as well; a general trans display should have all sorts of trans and gender variant people represented. Here are some trans-specific display ideas to start with:

- Any books on trans and gender variant topics (especially if your collection is on the smaller side)
- Books by openly trans and gender variant authors, whether the subject matter is trans-related or not
- Young adult or children's books with trans and gender variant characters
- Memoirs and biographies of trans and gender variant people
- Myths and facts about gender identity

- Movies with trans and gender variant characters
- Books focused on particular intersections of identity (such as trans women of color or trans people with disabilities)
- International Transgender Day of Visibility (March 31)
- Transgender Awareness Week and Transgender Day of Remembrance (November 20 and the preceding week)

Trans resources should also be included in other displays and lists. As books by black authors should not show up only in February, books on trans topics should be included wherever they are relevant. This is another way to demonstrate that your library respects and supports trans and gender variant people at all times. It also demonstrates that trans and gender variant people engage with the world in ways not solely defined by our gender identity. If you have trouble finding trans materials for a given topic, consider adding to your collection. Here are some ideas for displays that should include trans and gender variant content:

- Pride Month (June, celebrated in April on some college campuses)
- Black History Month
- Women's History Month (include books about trans women but not trans men or nonbinary people)
- Romance novels and other genre themes
- History (almost any topic probably has some trans-related content)
- Back to school/college
- Graphic novels
- Religion (there are many harmful books about trans people and religion, but there are also plenty of excellent ones)
- Local information, not necessarily books (such as documentation on how to get a legal name or gender change in your county, or directories of all-gender restrooms in the area)
- Everything else! Trans and gender variant people are part of every topic you can think of, and representation is integral to creating an inclusive community.

CATALOGING

My cataloging experience consists of a few courses and an internship during grad school. Therefore, this section will be more of a literature review than anything else; I highly recommend reading all of these publications for more detailed information.

Research on the effects of cataloging practices on trans and gender variant people can be divided into two main categories. The first is how catalogers describe gender as a topic. Angell and Roberto (2014) provide a brief overview of this issue. In an earlier article, Roberto (2011) critiques the limitations and inaccuracies of Library of Congress Subject Headings, Library of Congress Classification, and Dewey Decimal Classification when they attempt to describe materials about trans people.

The other category is how trans and gender variant authors are identified and described. A study of the name authority records of sixty trans authors found that 65 percent of those records outed the subjects, often in problematic ways (Thompson, 2016). Billey, Drabinski, and Roberto (2014) critique the original form of RDA Rule 9.7, which instructed catalogers in how to record authors' gender. Five years later, Billey and Drabinski (2019) report on a successful campaign to make the gender section more inclusive of trans and gender variant authors. Their webinar on RDA 9.7 and gender in cataloging is an excellent combination of basic queer theory and practical guidance (Billey and Drabinski, 2017). Like Thompson, they suggest ORCID-style uniform resource identifiers (URIs) as a possible solution to name ambiguity; as mentioned in Chapter 3, "Personal Information," I agree that this would resolve a lot of the issues that come up for trans and gender variant authors who change our names.

One full section of the book *Ethical Questions in Name Authority Control* (Sandberg, 2019) is devoted to trans and gender variant identities. One chapter uses the philosophy of language to point out the consequences of connecting legal names to names of use or pen names; it also talks about the problems that arise when the instructions for cataloging gender (and the harm caused to individuals when it is done badly) are not clear (Shiraishi, 2019). Another chapter discusses the harmful role of gender essentialism in cataloging and connects it to the pattern of violence against trans women and femmes of color in the United States (Polebaum-Freeman, 2019). Kalani Adolpho writes about the ways in which current cataloging practices continue to marginalize gender diverse people, especially those of Indigenous and non-Western identities. They emphasize self-identification and conclude that direct communication with an author, in which they clearly state how they want to be described with full knowledge of how that information will be used, is the only ethical way to catalog gender (Adolpho, 2019).

My personal noncataloger thoughts are that there is no reason to catalog gender that outweighs the potential for harm. There are any number of ways to disambiguate authors, and gender should not be one of them. As some of the scholars mentioned above point out, even the updated practices for gendering authors are deeply problematic. Accurately and respectfully recording gender takes knowledge of gender theory that few catalogers have, and it seems unlikely that this will become part of their standard training. It is far, far simpler to remove gender from records entirely. In general, I ask that catalogers simply remember that trans and gender variant people exist. Perhaps this sounds like a joke, but I actually mean it. Like many other elements of library work, transnegativity is probably not intentional, but systems developed from a cisgender perspective inevitably harm and erase trans and gender variant people.

QUICK FIXES

- Incorporate trans materials into displays and recommendation lists.
- Revise the collection development policy.
- Start discussions in cataloging and collection development departments about how to make your collection gender inclusive.

LONG-TERM SOLUTIONS

- Continually assess and improve cataloging practices for describing trans and gender variant topics and authors.
- Develop a collection representative of all different trans and gender variant experiences.
- Keep collection current by weeding outdated resources.

REFERENCES

Adolpho, Kalani. "Who Asked You? Consent, Self-Determination, and the Report of the PCC Ad Hoc Task Group on Gender in Name Authority Records." In *Ethical Questions in Name Authority Control*, edited by Jane Sandberg, 111–131. Sacramento, CA: Library Juice Press, 2019.

American Library Association. "Top 10 Most Challenged Books of 2017." American Library Association (accessed March 5, 2019), http://www.ala.org/advocacy/bbooks/NLW-Top10

Angell, Katelyn, and K. R. Roberto. "Cataloging." *TSQ: Transgender Studies Quarterly* 1, no. 1–2 (May 2014): 53–56.

Avery, Dan. "An Anti-Trans Book Is Topping Amazon's Gay & Lesbian Best-Seller List." *NewNowNext*, January 26, 2018. http://www.newnownext.com/an-anti-trans-book-is-topping-amazons-gay-lesbian-best-seller-list/01/2018/

Billey, Amber, and Emily Drabinski. "Cataloging, Gender, and RDA Rule 9.7." Webinar, Association for Library Collections & Technical Services, March 15, 2017. http://www.ala.org/alcts/confevents/upcoming/webinar/031517

Billey, Amber, and Emily Drabinski. "Questioning Authority: Changing Library Cataloging Standards to Be More Inclusive to a Gender Identity Spectrum." *TSQ: Transgender Studies Quarterly* 6, no. 1 (February 2019): 117–123.

Billey, Amber, Emily Drabinski, and K. R. Roberto. "What's Gender Got to Do with It? A Critique of RDA Rule 9.7." *Cataloging and Classification Quarterly* 52, no. 4 (2014): 412–421.

Lee, Traci G. "Being Transgender No Longer a 'Mental Disorder': APA." *MSNBC*, December 4, 2012. http://www.msnbc.com/melissa-harris-perry/being-transgender-no-longer-mental-disorde

Polebaum-Freeman, Hale. "Violent Cis-tems: Identifying Transphobia in Library of Congress Name Authority Records." In *Ethical Questions in Name Authority Control*, edited by Jane Sandberg, 155–179. Sacramento, CA: Library Juice Press, 2019.

Roberto, K. R. "Inflexible Bodies: Metadata for Transgender Identities." *Journal of Information Ethics* 20, no. 2 (2011).

Sandberg, Jane, ed. *Ethical Questions in Name Authority Control*. Sacramento, CA: Litwin Books, 2019.

Shiraishi, Naomi. "Accuracy of Identity Information and Name Authority Records." In *Ethical Questions in Name Authority Control*, edited by Jane Sandberg, 181–194. Sacramento, CA: Library Juice Press, 2019.

Simon, Carol. "Being Transgender No Longer Classified as Mental Illness: Here's Why." *USA Today*, June 20, 2018. https://www.usatoday.com/story/news/2018/06/20/transgender-not-mental-illness-world-health-organization/717758002/

Thompson, Kelly J. "More Than a Name: A Content Analysis of Name Authority Records for Authors Who Self-Identify as Trans." *Library Resources & Technical Services* 60, no. 3 (2016).

Conclusion

I am writing this section, appropriately enough, on Transgender Day of Visibility 2019. With that in mind, I want to point out one of the common threads you may have noticed throughout this book. There are all sorts of ways in which libraries actively or passively reject trans and gender variant people. Many of these have to do with visibility—or rather, complete lack thereof. All of the standards and systems that ground our profession were developed with the assumption that everyone who would ever work in or use a library would be cisgender (not to mention heterosexual, white, and abled). The issue is very rarely that individual library workers today are transphobic, though some are. It is that marginalized identities remain so invisible that the problems never occur to the people with power to solve them. So that is what I am asking readers to do. Take tools from this book or make your own, but remember that we are here. We are your coworkers, your students, your teachers, your patrons. This work is feasible, but we need your help to do it.

QUICK FIXES

- Remember that trans and gender variant people exist.
- Take steps to make your library safe and welcoming for people of all genders.

LONG-TERM SOLUTIONS

- Dismantle the gender binary.
- Create an equitable society.

Glossary

Note: The terms here are limited to the ones used in this book. For a more comprehensive list of the language used to describe trans and gender variant people, look at the Trans Language Primer (https://www.translanguage primer.org/). This excellent resource is regularly updated and is created by trans and gender variant people.

AFAB: assigned female at birth

Allyship: behavior that supports people of marginalized identities

AMAB: assigned male at birth

Cis: abbreviated form of "cisgender," pronounced like "sis." "Many cis librarians have never thought about the needs of their trans and gender variant patrons."

Cisgender: having a gender identity that matches one's gender assigned at birth. "I am transgender; my brother is cisgender."

Cisnormative: treating cisgender people as the norm and all others as anomalous

Come out: as an LGBTQ+ person, to share one's sexual orientation, romantic orientation, or gender identity with another person or group. "I came out as transgender to my employer."

Gender binary: the false idea that everyone is either exclusively male or exclusively female

Gender identity: a person's sense of their own gender

Intersectionality: the concept that people of multiple marginalized identities, such as trans black women or nonbinary people with disabilities, face increased difficulties because of the multiple forms of societal oppression enacted against them. (This term was originally coined by Kimberlé Crenshaw to talk about African American women.)

Legal gender: the gender on a person's driver's license or other legal documentation

Legal name: the name on a person's driver's license or other legal documentation

LGBTQ+: umbrella term for people who are not straight or cisgender. Acronym for lesbian, gay, bisexual, transgender, queer, and more (includes asexual, aromantic, intersex, and other identities)

Misgender: to indicate that someone is of a gender that they are not, often by using the wrong pronouns. "The supervisor accidentally misgendered the new circulation assistant."

Mx.: honorific, usually pronounced like "mix." Gender-neutral equivalent of Mr. or Ms.

Name of use: the name a person uses for themselves and wants others to use for them

Nonbinary: (1) a gender identity that is neither male nor female. "The systems librarian is nonbinary." (2) an umbrella term covering all identities that are not within the gender binary, including genderqueer, genderfluid, and others. "Our application is designed to include nonbinary people."

Out (adjective): for an LGBTQ+ person, to be open about one's sexual orientation, romantic orientation, or gender identity. "I am out at work but not to family, so please be careful when you meet my parents; I don't want them to know that I'm trans."

Out (verb): to disclose someone's sexual orientation, romantic orientation, or gender identity without their consent. "The school outed the trans student by putting their legal name on class rosters."

Trans and gender variant: umbrella term for people who do not fully identify with the gender assigned to them at birth, including transgender, nonbinary, agender, genderqueer, and genderfluid people, among others

Trans man: a man who was assigned female at birth

Trans woman: a woman who was assigned male at birth

Transnegative: contributing to a negative experience for trans and gender variant people, often unintentionally

Transphobia: fear or hatred of trans and gender variant people

Resources

GENERAL INFORMATION

- *The Trans Language Primer* (https://www.translanguageprimer.org/)
- MyPronouns.org (https://www.mypronouns.org/)
- Shlasko, Davey. *Trans Allyship Workbook*. Think Again Training, 2017.
- James, Sandy E., Jody L. Herman, Susan Rankin, Mara Keisling, Lisa Mottet, and Ma'ayan Anafi. *The Report of the 2015 U.S. Transgender Survey*. Washington, DC: National Center for Transgender Equality, 2016.
- The Safe Zone Project (https://thesafezoneproject.com/)

ORGANIZATIONS AND GROUPS

- National Center for Transgender Equality (https://transequality.org/)
- Transgender Law Center (https://transgenderlawcenter.org/)
- Trans Lifeline (https://www.translifeline.org/, 877-565-8860)
- Gay, Lesbian, Bisexual, and Transgender Round Table of the American Library Association (http://www.ala.org/rt/glbtrt/)

FOR EMPLOYERS

- Human Rights Campaign. "Transgender Inclusion in the Workplace: Recommended Policies and Practices." https://www.hrc.org/resources/transgender-inclusion-in-the-workplace-recommended-policies-and-practices
- Kermode, Jennie. *Transgender Employees in the Workplace: A Guide for Employers*. London: Jessica Kingsley, 2017.
- Sheridan, Vanessa. *Transgender in the Workplace: The Complete Guide to the New Authenticity for Employers and Gender-Diverse Professionals*. Santa Barbara, CA: Praeger, 2019.

RESTROOMS

- Occupational Safety and Health Administration. "Best Practices: A Guide to Restroom Access for Transgender Workers." https://www.dol.gov/asp/policy -development/TransgenderBathroomAccessBestPractices.pdf.
- Sandberg, Jane. *Gender-neutral Bathrooms in Libraries*. GLBTRT Resources Committee, 2014. http://www.ala.org/rt/sites/ala.org.rt/files/content /professionaltools/bathrooms%20brochure%20for%20viewing.pdf
- Schwartz, Meredith. "Inclusive Restroom Design." *Library Journal* (May 8, 2018).

LANGUAGE GUIDELINES

- Kapitan, Alex. *The Radical Copyeditor's Style Guide for Writing about Transgender People*. Radical Copyeditor, August 31, 2017. https:// radicalcopyeditor.com/2017/08/31/transgender-style-guide/
- White, Erin. "Trans-inclusive Design." A List Apart, May 9, 2019. https:// alistapart.com/article/trans-inclusive-design/

INSTITUTIONAL GUIDELINES

- CSUSM Trans & Gender Non-Conforming Task Force. *Report & Recommendations*. San Marcos, CA: California State University San Marcos, 2017. https://infomational.files.wordpress.com/2009/06/csusm-trans-gender -non-conforming-task-force-report-recommendations-2017.pdf
- White, Erin, Donna E. Coghill, M. Theresa Doherty, Liam Palmer, and Steve Barkley. *Gender-Inclusive Library Workgroup Report*. Richmond, VA: Virginia Commonwealth University, 2018. https://scholarscompass.vcu.edu /libraries_task/1/.

FOR LIBRARIES

- Adolpho, Kalani. *Gender Diversity and Transgender Inclusivity in Libraries*. Presentation, Joint Conference of Librarians of Color, Albuquerque, NM, September, 2018. https://drive.google.com/file/d/1R6UbIjoff0RjjXkBHKBb GRikbMvawGnt/view
- Garber-Pearson, Reed, Micah Kehrein, Sunny Kim, and Bean Yogi. *Reimagining Transgender "Inclusion" for Libraries*. Webinar from First Tuesdays, 2018. https://www.youtube.com/watch?v=-CwFstp-7NM
- Kehreim, Micah. "Improve Your Customer Service Skills: Go Gender Neutral!" American Library Association. http://www.ala.org/advocacy /diversity/odlos-blog/intersections-improve-your-customer-service-skills-go -gender-neutral
- Krueger, Stephen, and Miriam Matteson. "Serving Transgender Patrons in Academic Libraries." *Public Services Quarterly* 13, no. 3 (2017): 207–216.

- Roberto, K. R. "Passing Tips and Pronoun Police: A Guide to Transitioning at Your Local Library." In *Out Behind the Desk: Workplace Issues for LGBTQ Librarians*, edited by T. M. Nectoux, 121–127. Duluth, MN: Library Juice Press, 2011.

- Sandberg, Jane. *Transgender-inclusive Library Card Applications: Issues and Recommendations*. GLBTRT Resources Committee, 2015. http://www.ala .org/rt/sites/ala.org.rt/files/content/professionaltools/trans_inclusive_libcard _forms_for_viewing.pdf

- Smith-Borne, Holling. "Best Practices for Creating a Welcoming Environment for Transgender and Gender Non-Conforming Individuals in Libraries." In *Brick & Click: An Academic Library Conference*, edited by Frank Baudino, Kathy Hart, and Carolyn Johnson, 109–118. Maryville, MO: Northwest Missouri State University, 2017. https://files.eric.ed.gov/fulltext/ED578189 .pdf#page=116

CATALOGING

- Angell, Katelyn, and K. R. Roberto. "Cataloging." *TSQ: Transgender Studies Quarterly* 1, no. 1–2 (May 2014): 53–56.

- Billey, Amber, and Emily Drabinski. "Cataloging, Gender, and RDA Rule 9.7." Webinar, Association for Library Collections & Technical Services, March 15, 2017. http://www.ala.org/alcts/confevents/upcoming/webinar/031517

- Billey, Amber, and Emily Drabinski. "Questioning Authority: Changing Library Cataloging Standards to Be More Inclusive to a Gender Identity Spectrum." *TSQ: Transgender Studies Quarterly* 6, no. 1 (February 2019): 117–123.

- Billey, Amber, Emily Drabinski, and K. R. Roberto. "What's Gender Got to Do with It? A Critique of RDA Rule 9.7." *Cataloging and Classification Quarterly* 52, no. 4 (2014): 412–421.

- Roberto, K. R. "Inflexible Bodies: Metadata for Transgender Identities." *Journal of Information Ethics* 20, no. 2 (2011).

- Sandberg, Jane, ed. *Ethical Questions in Name Authority Control*. Sacramento, CA: Litwin Books, 2019.

- Thompson, Kelly J. "More Than a Name: A Content Analysis of Name Authority Records for Authors Who Self-Identify as Trans." *Library Resources & Technical Services* 60, no. 3 (2016).

Index

About the Author

STEPHEN G. KRUEGER (he/him or they/them) is the Access & Outreach Services Librarian at Randolph College. He holds an MSLS from the University of North Carolina at Chapel Hill, where he received the University Diversity Award and the LGBTIQ Advocacy Award. He writes and presents on how libraries and institutions can support trans patrons, students, and employees. Krueger was a 2018 American Library Association Emerging Leader. In 2017 he founded the Gender Variant LIS Network, a group for trans and gender variant library workers and students. For more information, go to www.stephengkrueger.com.